MW00444989

The Organizing Box

The Organizing Box

A Creative Yet Practical Solution

For Organizing Your Spaces

Jackie May

All names have been changed in order to protect the privacy of each individual mentioned.

Copyright © 2017 Jackie May

All rights reserved. No part of this book in any form may be used or reproduced in any manner whatsoever without prior written permission from the author. If you would like permission to use material from this book, please contact at TheOrganizingBox.com.

Author and Cover Photo Copyrights © 2018 Erica May
Cover Copyright © 2018 Erica May

ISBN-13: 978-1728736570

For hubby, who has

supported me since day one,

and our children and grandchildren.

For my mom.

Thank all of you for loving me and

believing in me.

Acknowledgements

Many thanks to Betty May, Julie Russell,
Johanna Eckenrode, Cathy Chapman, Cheri Sonnenberg and
the HHL Marketing & Publishing (MAP) group for your
feedback, support and encouragement.
I truly appreciate all of your time and suggestions
to make this book better.

Contents

PART I. GETTING STARTED

INTRODUCTION

WHY MUST LIFE BE SO HECTIC?

Finding time to declutter our spaces seems almost impossible. We want to live in orderly homes so we bombard ourselves with questions like: *Where do I start? What do I do with everything? How can I organize when I can't seem to find time to blink? Where do I find the time?* As these questions swirl around in our brains, we feel overwhelmed because we don't know the answers. We feel defeated and frustrated before we begin. So we do nothing. Or, if we make an attempt, we end up disappointed when we fail to succeed.

So back to our busy lives we go, operating on auto pilot. *Hurry up and do this. We're late, again. Answer the cell phone, return that text. Get dinner. Pick up the kids. Clean the house. The check engine light! Work overtime. Make the dentist appointment. Buy this new thing. Throw that there. Need to exercise. Accumulate.* On and on it goes. We

1

never seem to get much done but are always doing.

Recently, a friend told me, "One of the kids said all I ever tell them is to, 'Hurry up and help me straighten the house!' And yet it's still messy. I feel so bad because I know they are right. I feel so frustrated. Like such a failure. I can't seem to find any time to do the things I really need to. My home and life seem out of control."

My friend wanted a neat and orderly home. A home where she and those who lived with her could find things without hours of searching. Yet, she didn't have time to declutter or know how to go about it. I understood completely. Been there. Done that.

That is why I am excited to share this book with you. I know that it works because it worked for me.

The Organizing Box is a creative yet practical approach to organizing. It works using the same four steps in small spaces around your home. With this solution, you can finally gain control over your home. Really, you can. You will find that it will also help you identify and adjust any habits that are contributing to clutter.

While my friend craved orderly spaces in her home, her approach sabotaged her efforts. In her thinking, she was a victim of her disorder. Therefore, she had no choice but to live that way. It was important to her to know what was in each space so she could locate what she needed when necessary. But her method hadn't worked. She needed to know that there was a better and simpler way that worked with her instead of against her. She needed a solution that explained the basics of how to do it. She needed to understand how to **gather, sort, assign** and **maintain** the items around her home.

This is the way of *The Organizing Box*. Let's get started!

CHAPTER 1

A CLUTTERED TO ORGANIZED STORY

If someone showed up, unexpected, at your door, right this minute, would you be embarrassed to invite them inside because of the clutter?

What if someone asked to borrow a pair of scissors, would you be able to walk over to where the scissors are stored? What about a battery for the remote? Ok, do you know where the sales flyer from the mail is that you saved to look at today?

If someone had asked me those questions, several years ago, the answer would have been a firm, "No way." Maybe you know what I am talking about. Maybe you waste time looking for items that you know should only take you seconds to find. Maybe you know what it is like to feel shame over your cluttered home so you suggest meeting visitors somewhere else. Isn't that the reason why coffee shops were created?

Several years ago, every single space in my home (drawers, cabinets, dresser and countertops, tabletops, floors, under the beds) showed signs of disorder and chaos. The best word to describe the chaos is scattered. I mean REALLY scattered. Disaster may actually be a better word. I didn't even want to think about the amount of clutter. All I wanted to think about was the perfectly neat home of my dreams. The only problem with my dream was my lack of knowing how to make it real. My reality was that I was one of those people who had more possessions in my home than I could possibly keep up with.

Thankfully, over a period of time, my dream became my reality through my organizing box. It was a cardboard box where items from any small space were placed (this became the inspiration for this solution). Then, using what I call the "four sides" of the box—**gather, sort, assign and maintain**—in the small spaces around my home, I created and have maintained order. All in my own timing.

What I found most helpful about my box was the practical way it helped me order my home in the small amounts of time I had available. It also was a creative approach to the mundane and overwhelming task.

In this book, I will share with you the four sides and how they all work together. You will discover how to: **GATHER** the time to organize, along with supplies and items together into your own box; **SORT** through each item; **ASSIGN** a home to each item; **MAINTAIN** the order over time.

My box also helped me identify and adjust those habits that worked against me. In time, I achieved neatness.

The main reason I decided to write this book was to help others who, like me, are super busy yet cannot seem to find time to organize their spaces. It's also for those who have no clue where to start or how to go about it. It is intended to be a guide to help find the time and tools needed to create the home you want, one space at a time.

My Messy Story

The spaces in my home had always been untidy. As a wife and mom, I was already quite the VOM (Veteran of Messiness). Messiness was a war I had been battling for all of my adult years. In fact, my VOM status wasn't limited to my adult life. As a child, my bedroom held me hostage as I spent countless hours trying to "find" something that I knew I had somewhere.

I remember one time when I was about seven or eight-years-old. My aunt gave me a Mickey Mouse necklace from Walt Disney World. I adored that necklace. However, the first time I wore it the clasp broke. Saddened and angry, I decided that my dad could fix it. So what did I do? Well, the logical answer would be that I walked out to the living room, told my dad the story and asked him to fix it. Yep, that would be the logical answer. Instead, I threw it into a drawer. The emotional attachment to the item was already in my heart. It would soon become the reason I would keep anything and everything. I do remember feeling if I asked my dad to fix the necklace, he might chide me for breaking the new gift. Also, I felt that to throw it away would be like throwing my aunt away, since she bought the gift for me. I know, it's crazy for a child to think that way but my mind was already beginning to practice letting wrong thoughts toward my possessions take hold. So what choice did I have in my seven or eight-year-old mind? The only option I could see was to put it in the drawer.

That way of thinking continued year after year. Whenever my mom would tell me to clean my room, my "cleaning" became tossing things underneath my bed: toys, games, puzzles, clothes, clean or dirty, and just about anything else you can think of. The sad part of the story is that I never outgrew this way of cleaning the spaces I was responsible for. In fact, the more I collected over the years, the more I stuffed. Even my drawers didn't escape the expert pushing which helped me cram clothing into the drawers. When I would attempt to pull out a sock (which was never in a pair) from a drawer, everything else would fall out onto the floor. It took me twenty minutes to find two socks that were at least the same shade of white.

When I became a teenager, it was worse. My clothing was bigger and I had more items to store. However, as a teen, my packrat habits started to become a little embarrassing for me when friends would come over to visit.

"Hey guys, let's listen to the new record I got last week!" I would announce with enthusiasm.

"Okay, where is it?"

"Umm, yeah, well, maybe we can do something outside instead!" My face would turn the bright shade of red I would grow accustomed to.

Even today, my brother still likes to remind me, the way brothers do, of the disaster my room was when we were growing up. I can't seem to remember his room being that bad, so I just have to laugh with him, through clenched teeth of course.

Then, I met the man of my dreams. I had never lived alone in my own place before marriage and my groom was a military man who had already lived in the barracks. The US Army supplied most everything he needed. This meant that neither of us had furniture or a lot of things to start our new life together. We decided that we could use just about everything to furnish our new, little apartment. This proved to be no problem due to the generosity of both our families. We soon inherited many "new to us" items. I think both sets of our parents saw our marriage as a time to purge their homes to give us what they thought we would need and they did not want anymore. Of course, we wanted to buy some things we could call our own together. In no time, our two-bedroom apartment became a one-bedroom apartment with an extra room just for storage.

Fast forward a few years to the birth of our first child. This meant more and more items, many of which were obtained at garage sales, sales at baby stores and through many gifts given to us. Of course, a child needs toys, clothes and everything else, so the amount of stuff we owned began to accumulate like rabbits in spring. However, in the midst of all this collecting over the years, I had never changed the habits of my childhood stuffing syndrome. I hadn't gotten rid of anything either, so my house seemed to be bursting at the seams. Everything took longer to find than was necessary since I couldn't remember where I had last seen things like scissors, a pencil or my favorite pair of jeans.

I remembered how, as a child, I would get into trouble with my parents for my messy room. Now, as an adult, I felt like a substandard housewife and mother because of my pack rat habits. I knew that God was a God of order, not disorder. After all, He created everything to be orderly (the seasons, our heartbeats, the cycle of life and me—just to name a few) which is probably the main reason why I craved order and peace in the middle of disorder and chaos. Instead of being thankful for the things God had blessed me with, I resented the "things" because of the clutter. I felt unhappy and angry which led to anxious thoughts, short tempers and shame. It was embarrassing to have people over because my messy home didn't reflect the peace and joy that I wanted to convey to visitors.

I was not the only one trying to find things in my home. My family, also, suffered from the lack of neatness. We became experts at playing hide and seek with our possessions. Soon we added another child which meant even more stuff than before.

I was so distraught and so stressed by the mess at home that I decided enough was enough. My environment had become so cluttered that I felt completely overwhelmed. I didn't even want to be in my own house. As a wife and a mother, I was and still am, a very busy person. I felt there was no time to do all the work that it would take to fix the disarray I had on my hands. But, I realized that I had to do something for my family's sake and for my own sanity. Something besides renting a storage unit where I could move everything. The more I sat around my home, the more depressed, angry and frustrated I became.

Through my struggles I had a "perfectly" organized friend. At least in my mind. She had the tidy home I craved. It wasn't like a museum, where no one was allowed to touch anything. She didn't have every can facing the same direction and alphabetized. She just made her nest a livable, neat place to be.

Anyone who walked into her house felt at rest. Her orderly home resonated relaxation and peace. Each time I visited her, I felt at ease. I loved the way every item in her home had a particular space where it was kept.

If I needed a pair of scissors to cut a string off my shirt, I knew just where to look; in the top right drawer of her desk on the left side. I could get the scissors out, clip the string and return them to their place. It seemed so simple. Whenever I spent time at my friend's haven, I imagined how it felt to be clutter free. Each time I left her house, my reality would set in as soon as I opened my own front door. As I walked in, I chided myself, "Why didn't I just borrow her scissors to use here? I can't even find the three pair that I have somewhere in this house." I had bought the other two pair of scissors one at a time because I wasn't able to find the pair I knew was hiding somewhere. I was embarrassed by my home, which reflected my life. I vowed to somehow become organized (which seemed as impossible as trying to change my eye color). The only problem was; I didn't know how I would do it or where I would possibly find the time. I needed a simple and quick way to achieve my goal. I needed a way to find the time along with not having to buy a bunch of expensive equipment (closet shelving, bins, space makers, etc.) or hire a professional.

Realizing that it was no secret to my perfect friend that I needed help decluttering, I decided to see exactly how she kept things in order. I began to watch how she handled messes and where she placed her possessions. I asked many questions about how and why she did each thing. She patiently answered my questions, which gave me great ideas to implement. Her favorite saying to tell me was that the more you have to keep cleaned and organized the more you must clean and organize.

However, as I watched and questioned, I noticed one problem for me that she didn't have. The issue was time. Since my friend was a stay-at-home wife and didn't have any children at home, I figured a large part of her success was due to lots of time to work on it. As a wife and mother of two young children along with working part time, I didn't have all day each day to work on getting things in order. Finding extra time to do this seemed out of the question.

As I took my notes home with me from the day of my training, I wondered how I could make this work. I liked the way she kept only what she needed. I liked how she had a particular spot for each item and then placed it back there when she was done using it. I questioned how to implement what worked for her along with what might work for me. I realized to make my attempt a victory, I needed to take elements of what worked for her (since I really liked what she did, as well as her success) and experiment with what worked best for me. Then I could combine our two ways into an effective approach.

It was important to see immediate results from my efforts yet also find time to organize without sacrificing my family time or relaxation time. Looking at my habits and the way I spent my days, I noticed pockets of time during the week that could be used to declutter. Yes, I was busy but there were still little chunks of time where I could work on a very small area. So, I decided to experiment with a small space first. The overstuffed piano bench in the living room seemed a great starting point. Finally, I had a plan to approach the clutter in my home and it thrilled me. Despite my excitement, the work and many changes it would involve frightened me.

Facing my fears, I decided to tackle the challenge head on. I decluttered small spaces in little bits of time while tweaking my friend's methods to fit my lifestyle. That caused me to form this creative yet practical solution to disorder in a time limited, easy to follow pattern.

Organizing every single space in my home took about a year to complete. Although finishing the entire task may seem long, I discovered the benefit of working within my own timing. You see, over the course of a year, I not only succeeded with my goal but I also firmly established good habits and a routine that worked its way into becoming part of my everyday life. *The Organizing Box (TOB)* had worked. In fact, some of my friends noticed my transformed home and asked me how it happened. As I showed them the concepts learned, I was able to celebrate with them as they looked around their own newly tidy spaces. They knew the items in each one and where to find things, all within their time frame.

My hope in sharing my experience with others, who are fed up with the disorder where they live, is to show how this new approach can fit around a busy lifestyle. I want to help you experience the excitement and peace that results from an orderly home. In the following chapters, you will learn how to use *TOB*. You will also learn how to reuse *TOB* to see all your spaces completely changed.

When you first organize, you will see progress in a short period of time. With *TOB*, you will not have to work at it for an entire month before you are successful. You will see results the very first time you use it. *TOB* fits in your own schedule as you work one space at a time. This amount of time you have to tackle each mess determines how quickly it will be completed.

To help explain how *TOB* works, let me illustrate with

something that most people can relate to. I carry a purse that tends to become a "collect-all, carry everything around in it except the kitchen sink" kind of thing. My husband carries a wallet and has similar issues. He puts receipts, business cards, reminder notes and other various items in it. The problem lies in what to do with all the items we have collected in our purse or wallet after a period of time. I know that my husband and I tend to put off clearing either one out as long as possible. You would think that the purchase of a new purse creates a perfect opportunity to clean out my old purse then transfer everything fresh to the new purse. However, it usually does not. Instead, I remove only the items I want from the old purse and place them into the new purse. The other junk that's left in the old purse? Well, it's kept "stored" in the old purse. Then I stuff the old purse into a closet figuring that someday I will clean it out. Conveniently, I forget about my "storage" purse. My new, neat purse is the focus of my attention for the next couple of days, as I watch it soon become cluttered again like the old one.

I am not alone in this crazy way of organizing. At Christmas, my hubby received a new wallet. I watched as he sat at the table, transferring things to the new wallet. He chose to leave several things in the old wallet. A few days later, I found the old wallet sitting in a drawer.

However, at some point in time, due to a lack of a new purse, I have to clean out the current purse. It's true that cleaning out a purse is much easier than attempting to clean out an entire house simply because a purse is a smaller space. Why? Because my purse already contains the items which need to be decluttered.

Once I decide to clean out my purse, I know I need to *gather* together some time to do so (I usually give myself about a half hour). Then I need to *gather* together all of the items to be cleaned out (which is easy since they were already together in my purse). Next, I must *sort* through each item in my purse taking a mental inventory of the items within. I remove each item, decide what I want to keep and what I want to get rid of. After trashing the unusable items, I *assign* a place for each item I sorted. I then choose what items will go back into my purse. Some things don't even belong in my purse so I find a place for them somewhere in my house. The process is completed when I replace the items assigned to my purse back into it. Finally, all that is left is *maintaining* the tidiness.

TOB is similar to how a purse or a wallet is put in order; however, with *TOB* you will use a physical box to help gather your items together. Then you will clean out and clear out each space. The four sides that figuratively help "support" *TOB* are just as in the purse example above:

Gathering—finding time and items to organize,

Sorting—going through contents,

Assigning—finding a place for your items,

Maintaining—keeping up with the order and decluttering.

Then, using *TOB*, you repeat these steps in the next small space with the time you have available. This is how you will attain a neat and orderly home no matter how busy you are. Let's face it, most of us would describe ourselves as busy.

Think about it, how often have you bumped into someone you haven't seen in a while and asked, "How are you?" only to hear the answer, "Busy"? You probably gave the same answer when they tossed the question to you.

Americans are a busy bunch, that's for sure. You only need to look around to realize that you aren't the only one who never seems to have enough time in the day to do all the things that need to be accomplished, much less the things you would like to do. Someone once said that the more time saving devices we have the less time we seem to have. It's true, life is busy. Trying to find spare time seems nearly impossible. But we make time for the things we desire most and getting organized is at the top of that list. It will definitely be worth the time spent now if only to enjoy the time saved later in looking for lost or misplaced items.

Even if you can only free up an hour or so in your busy week to use *TOB*, you will be amazed and pleasantly surprised at the results.

The best way to use *TOB* is to read this book through, then go back to implement what you've learned. You can use *TOB* in any space that is cluttered. That means any that are inside or outside of your home, your office, church or place of business. The purpose of *TOB* is not only to show you a creative yet practical way to clear clutter in a short amount of time; but to show you what to keep and what to give away. It will show you how to organize what you choose to keep then how to stay that way. As you watch *TOB* change your messy places into neat places, you will be motivated. You will know what items you own and where to find them.

For quick reference, you will find a summary of the chapter's main points at the end of each chapter.

I am happy to be with you on this journey. You should be

proud of yourself for being willing to take on this challenge. Remember, you can do this and it will be worth it when you see what you are capable of. So, are you ready to see how *TOB* will transform your home or other current messy space? If you are, I can't wait to show you *TOB*!

CHAPTER 1 SUMMARY

✓ *TOB* is a creative yet practical approach to organizing the small spaces within your home one space at a time according to your schedule

✓ The four sides that support *TOB* are:

1. Gathering
2. Sorting
3. Assigning
4. Maintaining

✓ Read through the whole book before you begin

CHAPTER 2

THE BASICS OF *THE ORGANIZING BOX*

My friend, Mandy, is quite the expert gardener whether she is growing flowers, fruits or vegetables. She loves for her hands to be in the dirt nurturing plants until they produce their particular treasure for her.

I can appreciate Mandy's green thumb since I seem to kill most plants that get in my path. Yet, even though gardening may not be my strong suit, you and I both know the basics of how the planting process is supposed to work. Seeds are planted into the ground which eventually grow, blossom and produce a flower, fruit, or vegetable.

In order to grow your desired plant, five things are necessary: a seed, soil, water, sunshine and ongoing care. No matter what you happen to be planting, you must follow these steps: prepare the soil; plant, water and fertilize the seed; make sure the seed gets enough sunlight; then tend to any weeds that try to smother the plant. It doesn't matter if you grow a daisy or a watermelon; the planting pattern is the same.

With gardening, it is understood that time is required in order to see the rewards of your labor. Any gardener understands that continued care for a plant will produce a rewarding finished product. Your hard work, patience and care becomes evident as you follow a specific pattern of steps to nurture a flower, fruit or vegetable from a little seed.

Organizing your home successfully is similar to gardening. It works best when following and applying the pattern of *TOB* to all spaces of your home.

If you wanted to explain to someone the basic instructions, steps or pattern of planting and growing a plant from a seed, you would give them the simple steps with some possible variations depending on the specific needs of the plant. The pattern will always be the same since a plant is relatively universal in the way it must grow. In the same way, by following *TOB*, you will see your spaces become and stay orderly.

Organizing at your own pace is important as you see one small success at a time. This is a different way of looking at clearing out clutter. In the past, you may have approached the task as though it were only fit for those who were naturally neat and seemed to know where to place everything. However, with *TOB*, if you have ten minutes to work at it, then you do it for ten minutes. If you have an hour, then dig in for an hour. The key is not whether the process comes naturally to you, but the key is in using the time you have available to declutter. If you are busy (or if you're not busy), organizing small spaces this way makes sense and is doable. Even though the places we get into order may be small, don't overlook their importance. Think back to the example of how we clean out a purse or wallet. When we make the small space of a purse or wallet neat, it is not noticeable to most people but we sure notice it. Why? Because we use it so often. Also, after the purse or wallet is tidy we are able to find the items we need because we know what is inside. The results of cleaning out the purse seem almost immediate compared to doing an entire room. That is because the area we have to fix is much smaller than a whole room.

This knowledge becomes a powerful motivator to tackle small spaces verses larger ones like a bedroom or kitchen. Once we are able to experience success quickly in a small space, we are encouraged to continue on to the next until a room or area is completely finished, *one at a time*. Experiencing such early victory will also motivate you to continue using *TOB* in other places within your home until that final one is completed.

Organizing at your own pace works perfectly since you will see progress each day. Yet, you still will be able do the seemingly thousands of things that need to be done like working, cooking, cleaning, grocery shopping, running kids to practice and trying to make time for yourself.

The way *TOB* works presents a different way of thinking. Instead of tackling your whole home or garage or whatever it is that you are aiming for, you only need to use *TOB* to tackle one specific space. After you finish that, you will move on to the next one when you have the time and are ready. Soon, this way will become something you don't have to think about HOW to do it, you will just DO it because you know the results. You will like the outcome.

CHAPTER 2 SUMMARY

- ✓ Organize at your own pace using whatever amount of time you have whether it is ten minutes or two hours
- ✓ You will use *TOB* on one small space at a time

CHAPTER 3

WHERE TO ORGANIZE FIRST

Before using *TOB*, it's vital to decide what will be organized first.

A few years ago, on Christmas Eve, our family car ran till it could run no more. Its final run happened to be right in the middle of a busy highway, as I was driving. It was done. Thankfully, we were able to pull off the side of the road until it was towed away.

This left my husband and me scrambling to find a reliable car for our family as soon as possible. The questions began, do we get a new or used vehicle? An SUV or a car? What is our budget for this unexpected purchase? Where do we begin looking?

It was overwhelming to think of all the options available to us. We needed to narrow what we would be searching for before we began the hunt. Looking at our budget and what would fit our family's needs, we decided to look for a new vehicle and the maximum total cost we would pay. Knowing our goal helped to focus us. Our maximum cost was not very much, which limited even more the selection of vehicles available from which to choose. After searching for two solid days, we found a new car at a price within our budget that worked for our family. Operation Transportation Hunt was a success!

If we hadn't decided ahead of time what type of vehicle and the maximum cost, our search would have been too broad. We couldn't have found the car we needed without a lot more stress.

Similarly, to begin our task, we must know where and in what space we want to organize before we can begin the decluttering process.

For some, choosing this place, especially in the beginning, can be overwhelming. But it doesn't need to be. A good way to figure out where to begin is by understanding *TOB*'s approach to starting in a small space (just like the purse or wallet can be called a small space).

Starting in this way is the entire point on which *TOB* is based. Each "small" space that you choose is really a breakdown of all the **areas** and **rooms** within and around your home. The small spaces are literally the smallest spaces in those **areas** and **rooms** within your home that contain stuff.

For instance, an "area" (which is usually considered large and open) around your home could be:

A garage

A shed

The attic

A hallway

The basement

Stairs

A landing

While "rooms" (these can be large or small but are usually considered smaller than an area) within your home could be:

A bedroom

A living room

A dining room

A kitchen

A family room

A bathroom

A closet

The "small spaces" we are talking about (which are what we will be organizing) could be:

Drawers

Shelves

Cabinets

Countertops

Tabletops

Underneath beds or couch

Plastic totes or boxes

A single step

As you can see from the examples listed, a "small space" (where we would use *TOB*) is anywhere stuff is placed, shoved or kept in your home.

The first small space I would recommend choosing is any inside a little area/room, such as a drawer in a bathroom, a single shelf in a closet, a drawer in a desk, underneath a couch in a living room, a step on a set of stairs, etc. By choosing a place like this within a little area/room first, you will be able to see the entire area/room organized quicker than if you tackled a space within a larger place. Less time will be needed to do a smaller area/room compared to a larger area/room. Don't forget that the sooner you can physically see and experience an entire area/room that is tidy you will be encouraged and motivated to continue on with the rest of your home. For instance, if you choose a drawer in the kitchen to do first, it may take longer to organize the entire kitchen than it would a bathroom or a closet. This is simply due to the fact that there are many smaller spaces in a kitchen compared to a bathroom or closet.

The first room I chose was the living room. Our living room was not very large. It consisted of mostly furniture with no closet. The spaces where clutter loomed were in the TV stand, inside the piano bench, underneath the couch and inside a toy box. By beginning in a room everyone used, I knew my family and I would quickly notice the neatness of all the spaces within the room.

When I first organized my home, I chose to finish every space in the living room before moving onto the next room and so on. Completing each space in one room (instead of moving from one in a room to another in a different room) helped keep me on task. Working this way motivated me to finish all the spaces in the living room since I had a specific end in sight: an orderly living room.

However, when you use *TOB*, please do not feel that you have to declutter everything in a particular room before you move onto the next room. You may wish to do all the drawers in your home or all of the closets first. It doesn't matter where you use *TOB*. Just make sure that *TOB* works for you in the way that fits your end goals, works easiest for you and helps motivate you the most.

After you have decided in which room you will begin using *TOB*, you will want to decide the "space" in that room to organize. Remember, it could be a drawer like a junk drawer, a dresser drawer, bathroom drawer; or it could be a shelf or floor of a closet; under the couch, or anything like that. It could be the top of a dresser, top of a counter, a table top or a corner where stuff has accumulated on the floor. The whole idea to remember is that you are going about this in bite size chunks, the small spaces in that room.

The reason I love tackling small spaces is that we are able to empty the entire contents of the space into a physical box and finish it quicker than a whole room. Just like a purse or wallet is easier to manage instead of an entire room since all the items are already gathered together into one place; *TOB* makes our task easier since we have gathered together all the items into a box. We will talk more about how to use a physical box in a little bit, but for now it is important to realize that there is a specific reason for choosing one small space at a time.

The first space I chose in my living room was the piano bench. Not only did this bench provide a nice hard seat for whoever played the piano but under the lid lay a hidden opportunity for all types of things to collect. In fact, there were so many items inside the piano bench that the bottom sagged from the sheer weight of the junk. The collect-all that the piano bench turned into happened from quick clean ups.

For example, if I found out that someone was going to be visiting, I knew I had to do a quick clean up of the living room. Any hidden spot became a place to toss and shove things. Particularly, the piano bench. If I couldn't shove anything else under the couch, then the piano bench was fair game for papers, wrappers, books, pencils, little toys, and socks. You name it, into the bench it went.

Let's now think about you and your home. What area or room would you like to see organized first? Remember to consider areas or rooms that have as few spaces as possible. Is it a bathroom? A closet? A dining room? The landing of the steps? You might want to take a little walk around your home to look for the right room to start. Once you find that room, look for a spot within that room.

Look for the smallest space within your room to begin. Once you identify it, you will declutter with *TOB*. Tell yourself that this is your first time using *TOB*; you will get the system down. At the beginning, using *TOB* may seem mechanical as you are following step by step instructions (which you probably will) but with each new spot you finish, you will soon not need instructions. You will just know how to do it. You will be able to declutter each new one a little faster and easier.

After you have determined where you will begin, you may sense a bit of excitement nibbling at you to get started. But no matter how much you might want to jump in, hold on a bit longer until you hear how *TOB* is used to declutter. After that, it's all systems go!

CHAPTER 3 SUMMARY

- ✓ Decide which area or room you want to organize first
- ✓ Decide in which small space within the area or room you will start

PART II. USING THE FOUR SIDES OF THE ORGANIZING BOX

CHAPTER 4

SIDE 1: "GATHER" TIME AND SUPPLIES

Whenever you start any project like painting, scrapbooking, cleaning or something similar, the first and most important thing you can do is to gather together everything you will need to accomplish your task.

In order to use *TOB* effectively, you will need to gather three things: time, supplies and items.

If you have ever painted a room, whether to freshen it up, change the color or just because you love to paint walls, you will understand how this gathering together works. Before you actually roll the first pass of paint on the wall with that beautiful new color, you must decide (like gathering the time to organize) a day, an approximate time of day and for how long you plan to paint. Next you must grab (like gathering the supplies to help you) your paint, brushes, masking tape, plastic covers, etc. You also have to know which walls are to be painted along with which color they will become (like gathering the items from the space). This gathering together of everything is necessary preparation in order to successfully paint your room.

It is the same way with organizing. The first step is to get ready by gathering together everything you need to do the job. This is the first side of *TOB*—gather what you will use. Here is how you will gather the time, supplies and items.

Time

This process takes time, just like painting a room does, so it should be planned for in advance. After you know which room you want to paint, you plan a day to get your supplies together, then you paint. You wouldn't choose to paint a room if you didn't have the time to pick out then purchase the paint and supplies. You would also need time to tape off the woodwork, cover the floor, edges, then roll on the beautiful new color.

It's the same way with what we are doing. After you have chosen the small space you want to declutter within a room/area, think about what day and approximate time would be best to start.

Think about how much time you can realistically devote

toward using *TOB* in this space. Daily chores, family activities, work and many other things get in the way of achieving what we really want. That is why we must objectively look at the true amount of time we have available for this particular spot. Time will be on our side since we have chosen a small space to begin. That's a great thing!

Don't let finding the time to organize overwhelm you. You probably have more time to do this than you might realize. Look for bite size chunks of time in your day or week that fit into your lifestyle. Maybe you see that there are a few spots during the week where you are waiting for something, such as laundry to finish or your child to get done with his piano lesson. Maybe you can find time in the evenings while your spouse is watching TV and the kids are doing homework. Maybe it's during the day. Maybe it is right before you read a chapter out of your favorite book. The idea is to identify small chunks of time during your week where you could possibly fit in using *TOB*. You will not need to plan to use a whole day, weekend or week to begin using *TOB*. All you will need is to plan anywhere from a half hour to a few hours out of your day.

In Chapter Three, I mentioned that I chose the piano bench in our living room as my first space. Before beginning, I looked at my week to determine when would be the best time for me to begin. A couple of evenings in the upcoming week, our kids had a free night with no activities. Since that meant we would probably be eating dinner at home, I knew that my family had the habit, after dinner, to meander into the living room to watch TV or just hang out together. I saw this as the perfect chunk of time to declutter the piano bench. This time seemed ideal since the bench was in the living room where my family would be (so I could physically be in the same room as them) but instead of watching TV, I would be working on a different task. This was a perfect fit because my family could still do their thing after dinner yet I didn't have to miss out on being around them. So, I penciled in the day I would do the piano bench on my calendar, including the start and stop time. I treated this just as if it were a doctor's appointment I had to keep. That's when I began to get eager to start.

In the same way I found time to work on the piano bench, you might be able to find one particular day or time in an upcoming week to begin. For my first attempt, (in addition to the many other instances I organized each small space) finding time once per week or weekend worked great for me. But what happens if you can't find time that way? What if that doesn't work for you? It is no problem! What is so amazingly great about *TOB* is that you get to choose when and for how long you want to work. Your time can vary with each small space. It doesn't necessarily depend on waiting for a moment when you will be at home. You might be able to gather the time together every Saturday morning from 9–10am while sitting in your vehicle waiting for your child to finish gymnastic lessons. Or it might be while you are sitting at a soccer practice. The point is that gathering the time to work is easier than you think it will be simply because you aren't limited by WHERE you can work on it with *TOB*. Until now, when you have tried to bring some order to your home, you probably only did it when you were at home where everything was that needed to be organized. Not so with *TOB*. Since you will be decluttering one small space at a time, you are unlimited by where you can do it. We will talk about this more in depth when we discuss how to gather together the items you will go through. For now, know that gathering the time together doesn't need to be stressful. Don't necessarily look for a chunk of time when you will be at home, look for where there are any moments to use *TOB*, no matter where you are. Make sure to look for opportunities when you fill your waiting by playing games on your phone, checking out social media, reading a book or listening to the radio.

Another example of how I gathered time, that fit differently into my life than when I did my piano bench, is a plastic tote we use to store all of our receipts, important papers and bill stubs, etc. It needed to be decluttered. Looking at how I would gather the time together for the tote, I knew, due to my crazy schedule, I would now have to find the time in a different way than had worked for me in the past. Since the tote would take quite awhile, I looked at my calendar/schedule for the next month. There was one particular week where I could set aside an hour each afternoon, Monday through Friday, to take care of this space. So I penciled through the planned week the afternoon hour I would be busy with the tote.

Since we are talking about finding time to organize, please realize that in a perfect world, working for one hour each afternoon Monday through Friday with no interruptions would be the ideal. However, I certainly don't live in a perfect world and I know you don't either. Kids come home sick from school, your boss calls asking you to work the day you thought you had off, a friend whose car broke down texts to ask if you can pick her up on the highway. This is life. So don't sweat it when/if the time you have gathered together gets eaten up in a different direction. The whole purpose of doing this in advance is not to enslave you or make you feel badly if you don't do what you planned when you planned. The purpose of gathering time beforehand is to give you guidance, a direction to follow and a way to bring neatness to your space. Just know that interruptions may happen occasionally but it's okay because you can always re-adjust. You can find a new time.

While interruptions can happen, if they seem to happen often, you may want to rethink the day/times you are choosing. Remember that you want to treat your planned time as an appointment. After all, it really is an appointment with yourself to accomplish something that you have dreamed of for quite awhile. Treat it as an appointment that you don't want to break. If a friend calls to go shopping during your planned time, politely decline, knowing full well that working toward your goal will be well worth the sacrifice of missing out shopping with her.

It's important to make the most of every single opportunity in your day and week. Soon, you will begin to see all the ways possible to gather time together to fit organizing into your day.

Supplies

After you have gathered a day and time together, the next thing you will need to do is gather the necessary supplies.

Just as there are certain supplies needed for certain tasks, like painting, there are certain supplies needed to tidy up your chosen spot. In order to paint walls in a room, you need to gather your paint, a tray, brushes/roller, tape and something to cover the floor. These are the bare minimum supplies you need to paint. In the same way, to bring order, you need to gather a box, some bags, masking tape and a marker.

We finally get to talk about the most important supply you will need: a box that will serve as your very own organizing box. Your box is your most important supply since its major function is a "holding place" for each space's items. All items from the space you have chosen to declutter will be first emptied into this box.

So how do you go about choosing such an important supply? It's easier than you might think. I have found that the best type of box is an actual cardboard box or a plastic tote. My preference is a cardboard box for several reasons:

1. A cardboard box takes up less physical room— Whenever the box is not in use, it can be broken down for easy storage, then put back together with a bit of tape when it needs to be used again.

2. They are much cheaper than the cost of purchasing a tote (most often you can find them for free).

3. Usually it is lighter in weight than a tote which, once filled to the top with stuff, is much easier to lug around if needed.

Before you leave to look for a cardboard box, take a peek around, you might be able to find one without leaving your home. There may be one sitting in your house that is just the right size. Or perhaps a friend has one at his or her home that they would be willing to give to you.

If not, I would recommend going to your local grocery or retail store and asking if they have any boxes you can have. Some stores will send someone to the back to grab one that has been unpacked or is getting ready to be torn apart. You might want to call the store first to ask if they have any boxes that are not broken down already. Most stores break down their boxes as soon as they are unpacked but if you ask, they may be willing to keep one for you.

Another option is to visit a local moving, home supply or retail store to purchase a brand new box if that appeals to you more.

The size of the box is very important. You will want to make sure to choose a box that can be easily carried. Since you will be frequently using this box and transporting it around, you may wish to choose a box with cutout handles.

My suggestion would be to choose a box that is larger than a shoe box yet no larger than a microwave oven. If you choose a box that is too big, it will be too heavy to carry once it is full. If it's too small, you won't be able to place enough inside it.

After you have chosen your box, you will need to prepare it to use. Cut any lid flaps from the top or tuck them down inside your box. You do not want to be able to close the box. If you can close a box, you cannot see the contents. A closed box's contents are easily forgotten. For the purpose of organizing, closing up a box with stuff in it would be counter-productive to the ultimate goal. It means your box (which is meant to help you escape the clutter) once closed, becomes part of the clutter sitting in your garage, basement or closet. Like the saying goes, "Out of sight, out of mind." We don't want your box to become part of the mess; it is the way out of the mess.

You may have a plastic tote sitting around your house that is empty or not used for anything that you would like to use as your box. Or you might prefer to purchase a tote to use instead, which works well, too.

If you will be using a tote, then you will use these same recommendations when deciding which tote to use.

In addition to your box, you will need to gather together a few other supplies before you begin. Those supplies are: two trash bags, plastic grocery bags or a combination of the two; a roll of masking tape; and a marker like a Sharpie. My recommendation is to use what is already in your home.

One bag will be used for items that are trash. The other bag will be for items you will give away. Using the marker, write the words "Trash" and "Give Away" on two different pieces of the masking tape, then put one on each bag. This way you won't mix up which bag holds trash or which one holds give away items. You might want to use a white trash bag for one and a black trash bag for the other, it's up to you. If you do use different color bags, it's still a good idea to use the tape to mark which is which. The important thing is you don't get them mixed up when you are decluttering.

Once, I decided that I would organize the contents of a drawer while sitting in my car waiting for my son during his piano lesson. Before we left for his lesson, I grabbed my box full of the drawer's contents, then I pushed two plastic grocery bags into the top of the box. As he grabbed his piano books, he looked at me like I was a nut for carrying a full box out to the car. He just shook his head and didn't ask. After pulling into the piano teacher's driveway, he hopped out for his half-hour lesson. I parked the car, rolled down the windows and dug into the box as I waited. Going through each item, I began to toss some into the trash bag and some into the give away bag. After doing this for a minute or two, I noticed that trash items were mixed in with the bag of give away items. In the rush of grabbing the bags on the way out the door, I had forgotten to label both of them. That half hour piano lesson turned out to be more of a lesson for me to always remember to label my two bags.

After you have gathered your box and two labeled bags, take the marker to write on each side of the box. The four words you will write, one word per side, will be reminders of how to use it. On one side of the box write—GATHER; on the next side write—SORT; on the next side write—ASSIGN; then on the final side write—MAINTAIN. These are the four sides to *TOB*.

Now that you have gathered the time, along with the supplies you need to begin, you are ready to organize on the day and time you planned.

CHAPTER 4 SUMMARY

✓ Gather a day and time you will organize — treat it as an appointment

✓ Look for time wherever you can fit it in

✓ Gather a box or plastic tote

✓ Gather two bags, a marker and some masking tape to use

CHAPTER 5

SIDE 1: "GATHER" ITEMS

After you have chosen a time and a space, the next things to gather are the items from the place you will be organizing into your box. This is where the decluttering begins. You will want to take your box, bags and marker to where you have chosen, then place all of the items into your box. This part doesn't take much time.

Remove each item from the space then relocate it into your box, trash and all. Even if there are gum wrappers, don't take time to throw these away right now. This is not the time to rummage through each item, linger over or notice the items as you remove them from their current space then put them into your box. No matter how strong the urge is to stop to look at a particular item, you must resist doing so. It will only distract you from your goal and sidetrack you from getting to the next step. You will have time to look through each item during sorting.

It is important that you physically see the space you are working on emptied out and cleared off. If you are like I was, there might not be any place that is cleared off or empty in your home. That is part of what leads to the clutter. Everything is stuffed full, to the max. There is no room for anything additional because all the free space is taken up. It reminds me of our home computer. When we first purchased it, there was plenty of free space and the computer ran great. We could save all the data we wanted. As time went on, more programs, pictures and music were added to the computer, causing it to slow down. The same is true for your home. The more you add and fill up gives you that "slowed down" feeling. That is why it is imperative that you completely empty out each space you will be decluttering. It is an easy way to see a quick result which will inspire you to want to keep on keeping on. You will love the feeling that one orderly spot will bring to your heart, soul and home. Maybe, like me, you can't remember the last time you saw the bottom of a drawer, the shelf of a closet, the top of a dresser or countertop. This might seem like an insignificant detail but to actually see a space empty, no matter how large or small, is tremendously motivating, calming and peaceful.

After you have dumped the space's contents into your box, don't be surprised at the amount of crud you will find left over. No matter what has just been removed, you will most likely find dust, dirt, crumbs and pieces of who knows what laying or sitting where you just emptied out. No worries!

The very last thing you will do once you have gathered the items and transferred them to your box involves cleaning out the space. You will want to vacuum up, sweep or wipe down the crumbly leftover contents to make it clean, fresh and ready for the next step.

Something I did, that has worked well with drawers and shelves, was to place shelf liner on them. It has made the process of maintaining the neatness much easier along with helping protect the bottoms from spills and leaks. If you have shelf liner or something sitting around your home that you would like to use to line the bottom of the drawer, this is the time to put it down once the space is empty and clean. Maybe you have old wallpaper rolls gathering dust that could be used to line shelves or drawers or ask a friend if they have any old wallpaper. If they do, I bet they would be more than happy to give it to you to use. Many times, I have seen cheap wallpaper at yard or garage sales. Lining drawers or shelves is something that you don't have to do, it's just something that makes future clean up easier. It also takes the brunt of abuse from spills, scrapes and the like.

After you have gathered the items in your space, placed them into your box and cleaned, you may feel a temptation when looking at the full or overflowing box to think, "Maybe I will put this somewhere out of sight and deal with it sometime next year." Don't let that type of thinking into your brain. Be empowered! Be encouraged! You have taken the first step toward organizing. You are on your way to completing your entire home. Looking at a cluttered, full box can be overwhelming and may cause you to question whether or not you really want to do this. The important thing to remember here is this, yes; you really DO want to do this. This process is the first step in conquering the clutter bomb for good. This is just one step. It's not a commitment that you will do this to your entire home this week, this month or even this year.

It's important to address the possibility that may occur if all the items in the space do not fit inside your box. If that happens, there is no need for concern. Let's say you are gathering all of the items and transferring them to your box. The box becomes full so there is no way that you can possibly fit another item inside it. This will just take a little extra time but can easily be adapted. All you need to do is go on to sorting, even if there are items left in your space. The only thing that will need to be modified in gathering your items is that you will not need to clean, vacuum or wipe it down since there are still items left. Once you have worked through sorting the items currently in your box, you will then return to gathering the remaining items for round two. Then you will repeat through gathering and transferring into your box as many times as necessary so that eventually you can vacuum and wipe down the empty spot.

The way I would like to finish off this chapter is to encourage you that you are well on your way to starting a new way of living for yourself and your family. You may be wondering why I am getting so excited over such a little thing as this one space but the reason I smile, even just writing this, is because I vividly remember the day that I gathered my items together for the first time from the piano bench, cleaned it out then saw it clean and empty. It was thrilling (as well as encouraging) to look at that beautiful empty space and envision my entire home looking orderly.

CHAPTER 5 SUMMARY

- ✓ Transfer all contents from your space into your box

- ✓ Vacuum, sweep or wipe out the bottom of the space and if you desire, line it

CHAPTER 6

SIDE 2: "SORT" THROUGH YOUR THINKING

One Halloween, several years ago, my daughter returned from trick-or-treating and dumped the contents of her overstuffed bag of sweet treats on the kitchen table. As my husband picked through each piece, checking to ensure it was safe to eat, I noticed my daughter pushing the candy around searching with her little finger. She seemed to be looking for something specific so I continued watching to see what it was. She rummaged through the mess of candy until she found her target: The Tootsie Rolls. I watched as she picked up each Tootsie Roll and cleared an area on the table. She placed the Tootsie Rolls she had gathered in her little hand then plopped them in the cleared out area. Determined to make sure no Tootsie Rolls were forgotten or overlooked, she inspected the table one last time and picked up a few more she had missed. Then as she moved on to the Reese's Cups (I am making myself hungry) I asked her what she was doing. "Putting them all together," was her simple reply. I chuckled to myself as I realized that even in candy chaos land, order and organization is a nice thing to have even if you are dressed up like a princess.

I've been at parties where I have seen adults and kids grab a handful of M&M's to sort them by color. When I have asked why the need for color coded order, one's response was, "I like to eat my favorite colors first."

In the same way my daughter sorted out her Halloween candy, we will sort the items out of your box. However, before we begin sorting, it is important to understand two things about sorting.

First, sorting will be emotional. As you decide what items you will keep or get rid of, you will find that sorting will be the most emotionally challenging part of using *TOB*.

Second, sorting will consume the majority of time because sorting is where you will go through each item one by one to determine what you will keep, give away or throw away. Sorting is the nuts and bolts of *TOB*. It will take some thought and decision making.

As you get ready to sort and look at the contents in your box you will probably ask yourself, like I did, "How did I get so much stuff?!"

How Did I Get So Much?

One of the many reasons I had gotten myself into a disorganized mess was because I couldn't say no to anyone, especially to my extended family if they offered to give me something. It could be anything from a box of dishes, to clothes, to pictures, magazines, piano books, curtains, you name it. If someone offered it to me, I accepted it.

Another thing that I had a hard time saying "No" to was a good bargain. In fact, I loved getting a good bargain! It didn't matter if the bargain was at a garage sale, a book sale at the library, a clearance item at a department store or something similar. If it was a good deal; better yet, if it was free, I scooped it up.

Then, of course, there were all the things that people had given me as gifts over the years (knick—knacks, jewelry, cards).

However, the main reason I had "gotten" so much stuff was tougher to admit to myself. It was simply due to the fact that I had a difficult time letting go of anything that came into my possession.

In helping people bring order to their homes, I have noticed I am not the only person who has a tough time letting go of my stuff. After seeing others struggle with it and thinking about my own struggle, three reasons hit me why letting go was so difficult: 1) The inability to detach from possessions due to an emotional attachment, 2) The need to save an item for use in the future and, 3) Our belief that others will think of us as well off or more successful if we have an abundance of possessions.

Problem #1—Our emotional attachment to our possessions

Detaching from our belongings is often very difficult to do. It really doesn't matter why we feel the way we do about our possessions since the root cause in most cases is the same. Most people associate positive emotional feelings with certain or all of their belongings, which is how an emotional attachment to them can form. It is vital to realize that your possessions have nothing to do with the person who bought or gave the item to you or the feeling you may have about the item. The different items are just that, items. The important thing is to detach the item from the person or event that gave it to you.

This was a very freeing thought for me once I grasped hold of it. Realizing that these possessions of mine were just physical manifestations or representations of a person or event, not the actual person or event, helped me see that I did not just possess it, it possessed me. I wanted to keep it all but I realized a danger in wanting to keep more than we are meant to keep. Not only does it impact the state of chaos in our homes but it also impacts the state of chaos in our heart. Jesus spoke of this in Luke when He warned to be on guard against every kind of greed. He added that life is not measured by how much you own.

However, I also began to realize becoming clutter free did not mean that I had to get rid of every single item that meant something emotionally to me. What it did mean, though, was balance. The balance of keeping some items, but not every item that meant something to me. This helped ensure that I possessed each item yet it didn't possess me.

This is important to keep in mind because one of the side effects of this process is dealing with things that will evoke emotion and memories. It is vital to know that you will experience this side effect to determine in advance how you will handle it. That way, you can appropriately deal with those emotions.

I began to change my thinking toward the emotional hold my possessions had on me. Many, if not all of the items I agonized thinking of sorting through, were things that had significant emotional memories and feelings attached to them. A stuffed elephant that my oldest child loved to chew on when he was a baby, pictures that our daughter had drawn in kindergarten, letters my husband had written to me while he was fighting in the Gulf War, books my grandfather had given me and on and on I could go. The emotional connection I had to my possessions (which I discovered during the sorting part of *TOB*) was not something that I had anticipated.

I have come to realize that we have been blessed with so much, too much some might say, that not only our homes are stuffed to the brim but we have storage units packed full, too. We definitely have an emotional connection to our stuff when we are willing to pay money each month for a unit to hold it all.

Please note that the intention in this book is not to understand the how and the why of attachment or why so many of us with abundance have difficulty ridding our lives of any excess. There are many reasons behind the science of how and why we latch onto possessions, which we will not explore within these pages. But know that this emotional connection to what we own or the status, we may feel, owning a lot gives us is an extremely powerful force that needs addressing.

While guiding people through their clutter, I have seen tears shed over the state of their home. Some, out of frustration at not knowing where to begin and with themselves that they are continuing to contribute to their disorder despite their strong desire to change their environment. I have seen some shed tears because they knew that in order to become organized, they were going to have to part with items that they had grown attached to. It was actually painful to think of parting with anything in their home. I think that most, if not all, of us view our home as an extension of ourselves and the memories we have amassed over the years.

Think of all the memories you have accumulated within your lifetime, good and bad. Chances are that you have more memories than could fill the pages of a book. Let's just go with this for a minute or two. Think about one of the earliest good memories you can remember. Maybe it's a memory from when you were a little tike or perhaps the earliest good thing you can remember is back to high school. Whatever it is, sit with that one good memory. Remember sights, sounds, feelings and anything else you want about that positive memory. Did you need anything other than a gentle prod from me to remember that memory? More than likely, you were able to go back into the recesses of your mind to capture the time, the place, the sights, sounds, smells and feelings of that flashback. I hope that the good thought brought a smile to your face.

We could continue down memory lane if we wanted to and go on remembering hundreds of wonderful memories through the years. The point is that we were able to remember those things without the aid of a photo, a sight or an object. We were able to recall them simply from a suggestion to sit back and remember.

A friend, who was transferring to another state for his job, contacted me when he was readying to downsize. As he sorted and decided what to leave behind, he was surprised that he struggled with getting rid of some of his things. In particular, he had a stereo, which he rarely used, along with a set of bulky speakers that were over 20 years old. His problem with the stereo came to light when a co-worker offered to purchase the stereo and speakers. As my friend disconnected the speakers from the stereo he felt sadness thinking of not having the set anymore. To him, the stereo symbolized the beginning of adulthood and freedom since it was the first major purchase he had made on his own as an adult.

He had fond memories of listening to music loud and proud

with no one to tell him to turn it down. As we talked, I could hear the pain in his voice as he spoke of the paradox of emotions that hit him. He knew that he didn't need or even want the set anymore but was surprised that he felt such an emotional pull toward a stereo and a set of speakers. "It's going to be hard to get rid of things that I have kept for years. It's taken me a long time and a lot of hard work to accumulate all this," he confessed.

I felt his pain, "I bet it has. But at least you are following through selling the set. Remember you're making a good decision to downsize. It will be difficult. In fact, just count on it being difficult at first."

"I guess so."

I encouraged him to make certain that he was filling his mind with all the positive reasons of why he chose to declutter and ultimately downsize. He and his family would be moving to a smaller home. They didn't want to pay to store any excess. "And you can always focus on the fact that you are getting a nice chunk of change for the set."

He laughed, "Yeah, that's true. My co-worker is really happy to be getting it. She has been looking for a set like this for a while."

"It's probably like Christmas for her," I stated. "Think of all that space you will be clearing out."

Each time you rid yourself of something you don't use, you will feel more freedom and excitement. You will realize that possessions really don't define you. You are who you are because of the personality God created you with and your experiences. That's something that you can't downsize.

The memories we hold dear to our hearts are not attached to any object or item we have or could ever possess. A memory is in your brain and a part of you that goes everywhere you do. Like my friend, the memories he had of freedom or achievement are all felt or remembered because it is in his brain. He remembers fondly, he feels accomplished. Objects like the stereo and speaker set can help evoke his memories and emotions, but it is inaccurate to think that once the object goes away, those memories or emotions go with it.

You will also find that some items may cause emotional feelings that aren't necessarily driven by a particular memory. My fascination with history (in particular my own family history) caused me to face this issue when I began sorting my family room. My great, great grandfather built a log cabin in the 1800s that once stood on land that my family still owns. My great, great grandparents raised their family in the log cabin and great, great grandpa farmed the land around it. As time went on, one of his sons, my great grandfather, built a "modern" home across the road from the log cabin for his family which is still standing to this day. Recently, my mom went to the place where the log cabin once stood and found remnants of the fireplace. This would have been where my great, great grandmother cooked meals for her family. Where she undoubtedly dried the wet clothes of my ancestors. Where I'm sure the family gathered around in the evening for warmth and for light. In my mind, I like to think they gathered around the fireplace for stories and conversation about the war between the north and the south, which was happening at the time.

When my mom visited me after returning from her trip, she handed me a flat stone, about the size of a loaf of bread, and asked if I wanted it. She explained that the stone came from the remnants of the fireplace of the old log cabin. As I held the stone, I thought about the things this stone may have seen and heard. I thought that one of my ancestors had not only touched this stone but had taken the time to choose it, chisel it and fit it to become a part of the fireplace in his home. Suddenly, I felt an emotional connection to a rock! When visitors come into my home and see the stone sitting on the mantle of my own fireplace, the significance of the stone is lost unless I volunteer the story or they ask about it. Whenever I see it, I am reminded of where I came from and question if I look like any of them. The stone makes me wonder if I have the same facial expressions or laugh as any of them. To me, the stone helps represent me, who I am and my heritage.

There may be objects and items in your home that might not necessarily trigger a memory but they may represent something to you that you value beyond words. This is important to understand so that when you encounter these objects you will know how to handle those emotions. The exciting thing to know is that over time, these items will have less of a hold on you than they do now because just like the earlier exercise in bringing up a good memory, you will come to realize that since the memory is not within the object itself, the power of the objects over you will be lessened. Just like the stone on my fireplace, I can enjoy that connection through talks about my ancestors with my family and friends (who are kind enough to put up with it) without losing any connection in my mind or thoughts of them.

Become aware of what the items in your box really represent and that they are not all necessary to keep just so you can remember a memory, person or a connection. The important word in that previous sentence is the word "all". The freeing thing about choosing to think this way about the objects in your home is that those items will not have the hold on you they once had. You will be able to let a lot of them go. But realize that you don't need to let go of all of them. Once I realized this truly life changing truth, it was much easier to let things go that I would have never ridded myself of previously. In essence, you are giving yourself permission to let go of some yet still keep some. This permission became the catalyst in helping me to overcome my desire and perceived need to keep everything that represented a memory or had some type of emotional connection attached to it.

Having two children gave me the opportunity to have many memories attached to items that somewhat chronicled each of their childhood life stories. Both my son and daughter have made me various, wonderful treasures throughout the years. There are clay pots, Christmas tree decorations, pictures, bookmarks...you get my drift. I can think of one pot in particular that has a pipe cleaner flower coming out the top which my daughter made me for Mother's Day. How in the world could I get rid of these items knowing how much they meant to me? When I look at these treasures, I remember the kids at the age they were when they gave it to me. How could I let go of all this? The answer…I didn't. Those are a few of the treasures I chose to keep. I didn't list all the treasures I let go. Do you see what I mean? Giving myself permission to keep some, not all, freed me to enjoy the rest of the organizing process. My memories are still there and can be jogged back to my kids' younger days by looking at a few of the items, then putting them back where they go for another day. You don't need all of them.

This is huge. Make sure you tell yourself as you are decluttering that you don't have to keep it all but you don't have to get rid of it all either. Now, one thing that I want to clarify is that I am in no way saying you must rid your home of every single thing that is unnecessary unless you have an actual physical use for it.

I have kept some things that my family and others have given me, but the point is that I haven't kept every single thing they have given me. Right now, your possessions have gotten the best of you, plain and simple.

It's time to change your thinking before you begin sorting your box's items. You must change the tide and get the best of your possessions instead of the other way around.

Once I decided to bring order to my spaces, I knew enough was enough. I was ready to do what was needed to restructure my home. This included restructuring the way my mind thought about my possessions. As you declutter your home, you will find that you will be happier keeping a few items that hold sentimental value to you instead of keeping them all. The freedom you will gain from the ability to release your emotional connection with your possessions will be worth these beginning struggles. Once you can understand the emotional connection that your possessions have with you and decide that you will think differently toward them, you will be able to manage those emotions in a healthy and productive way.

The second problem I have seen why people have a difficult time ridding their home of excess is thinking that an item might be eventually needed.

Problem #2—We think we need to save items for later use

When Debra, a homeschooling mother, chose to organize the room she used to teach each day, it was for two reasons. First, it was the room that she spent the most time in during the day and secondly, it was the messiest room in the entire house.

As we began sorting through her items, I held up each item and asked her, "Is this something that you need?" It didn't seem to matter if it was a pencil, an empty tissue box, an egg carton or a completed math book, each time she would answer, "Yes, I need that."

"Why do you need the empty tissue box?" I inquired.

"I might need it for a project for Tyler," she answered.

"But you have three empty boxes on the floor! Okay, well what about the egg carton?" I suggested.

"Same thing, I might need it for a project."

"Okay…the math book, Debra. It's all filled in and you have no other children that will be in the second grade ever again. Why do you need this?"

"Well, I might need it as a math reference sometime."

This exchange with Debra was a perfect example of thinking we need to save things because we just might use them someday. Do you want to know what my answer was to Debra after asking those three questions? I asked her if she was going somewhere where she would never be able to get another tissue box. Or if it was somewhere where she would never be able to purchase eggs again. She smiled. She said of course she would buy more tissues and of course she would purchase eggs again. I asked her what type of reference she was so hoping to gain from the math book.

She thought about it for a second and said, "Well, in case I need to remember how the book taught him to add or if I want to review it with him, it will be there."

I said, "Okay, let's go with that. Let's make a folder for second grade review and tear out the last few pages of this book that summarize the concepts learned. Then let's put a few other second grade things that you are saving for the same purpose and you can condense all the finished second grade books into one folder. But, let's only do this IF you are sure you will use it. Have you ever reviewed the previous year's books before? Aren't the previous year's review concepts already at the beginning of next year's books?"

Debra thought, "Yes, that is true, and no, I haven't reviewed like that in the past but it is something that I really want to do. I would love to be able to review the concepts over the summer and then keep it going right into the fall."

"But Debra, realistically speaking, will you have the time to do this and have you done this in the past or is this just something that you think you might do?"

"Well, realistically speaking, every single year I have wanted to do that, but I haven't done it. But I would like for this year to be different," she admitted.

"Let's think of the best way to approach this from a realistic angle. If you do find the time to review with him, could you go online and find a website that might have games which would help him to be able to review the concepts or go to the library to see what review material is there?"

"Yes, I guess that is true," Debra paused.

"So we have two choices here," I pointed out. "We can make a folder, which will require time to go through each book then put the folder together. Or you can decide if you do find review time, you and Tyler can look online for review exercises or even hit up the library. Either way, you will be able to rid yourself of excess and open up this beautiful bookcase to store more things."

In the end, Debra decided to get rid of the tissue boxes, the egg carton and the math book. After they were gone, she didn't think about them again. Once summer came, she and Tyler were enjoying their time off so much; they decided not to think about school again until fall.

Sometimes, when we are saving an item for future use we are looking through rose colored glasses to see what we would like to do in the future. Often it's out of a fear that we will need something at a later time so we try to cover all our bases imagining the things that we will need. This "possible future use" thought is tricky because excuses to keep an item seem valid since we truly never know everything we will eventually need. This thought of saving something for future use can be fed when we find that we suddenly "need" something and so once we are able to find it stored away somewhere we think, "See, I am glad I kept that! I knew I would use it sometime." The trouble with this line of thinking is that as we collect more items than we may possibly need to use in the distant future, we rob ourselves of the simplicity and peace that exists within a tidy home now.

For example, Jennie, a wife and mother of two, had finally organized her home with the exception of the basement and garage which were the two places her husband Scott kept his things. "I don't know how to even begin to clear out his spaces," Jennie told me. "I just don't know what he really needs versus what he thinks he needs."

Jennie explained to me that Scott was quite the handyman and was extremely proficient at fixing most things around their home. He really enjoyed repairing what he could. Scott liked the fact that he was able to help his family by fixing things. He felt tremendous satisfaction that he was able to save his family the expense of service calls and materials since he practically had a do-it-yourself store in the basement and garage. However, both Scott and Jennie noticed that neither of them really knew what materials and supplies they had since there were too many items to find a place for. Also, the items they possessed were not in any type of order.

One day, when a plumbing pipe needed to be replaced, Scott began searching the garage and basement for tools and parts, which he knew he had, in order to replace the pipe. He had a general idea of where the parts might be. After some time, he found some pieces/parts that he needed (which he had saved for future use) to do the job but still needed more. Jennie was happy to see Scott excited to use some items he had saved for this "future use". However, Scott was not able to locate all of the items he needed to finish the job. Scott spent several more hours searching through totes and various shelves scattered around for some plumbing tape and a pipe cutter which he "just knew" he had. The end result after looking with no success? He went to the local do-it-yourself store, purchased plumbing tape and a pipe cutter.

Several months later, another job came along and as Scott was going through a box to get the equipment needed for the new project, he discovered the plumber's tape and pipe cutter (which he had originally searched for) hiding in a small, brown bag. So now, the couple had two rolls of plumber's tape and two pipe cutters. This not only cost them extra money but it created more things to store and go through every time a new project needed tackling.

Scott began to grow frustrated over the state of his basement and garage so Jennie enlisted my help in getting them on track. It was quite obvious that the amount of stuff Scott had accumulated could not be held any longer within the confines of the basement and garage. In fact, Scott had begun to find a place outside in the yard to start "storing" his future use items.

In the same way Debra realized that she didn't need to keep every tissue box for a possible future craft project, Scott needed to realize that he didn't have to keep every item but he could still keep some.

The key in learning how to stop thinking that every item must be kept for future use is to think realistically about what you will use based on past usage and future availability of the item. Meaning if you need it in the future, is this item something you can easily and cheaply obtain? Realize you can keep a little bit of most things just not all things.

Problem #3 — Thinking our many possessions make
us look more affluent or successful

We all care what other people think of us in some form or another. And to a certain extent, this can be a good thing. It's a good thing if we go to a job interview and think of the best way to dress or present ourselves in a way that the interviewer will like what we have to offer the company. We care what the interviewer thinks as they are interviewing us. Or when we purchase a gift for our child, we hope that they think we are giving the gift out of our love for them because we like to see them happy. We often spend hours searching many toy and department stores in order to find just the right thing. We care what our child thinks when they open the gift.

However, caring what people think concerning the amount of our possessions or lack thereof, is not a good thing. That which truly matters in life lies more in what we are willing to give away of our excess to those in need instead of holding onto that which we don't need just to attain status with others.

We need to learn to release the emotional attachment to our things, let go of thinking we cannot get certain items in the future and refuse to let other people's opinion of our possessions consume us. The way we got so much stuff is due to wrong thinking. Learn the secret of moderation. It will keep your perspective on your possessions realistic. Then these issues won't be stumbling blocks to obtaining and keeping an orderly home.

According to Webster, the definition of moderation is observing reasonable limits. Just like we all know that the healthiest way to live, eat, sleep and drink is to do so in moderation. This is the same concept for your home and all the stuff inside it. The best way to think about organizing is that it's okay to keep things but to keep them in moderation. Anything in excess is not what is best. Learn to just say no.

CHAPTER 6 SUMMARY

- ✓ Sorting will be the most time consuming part of using *TOB*
- ✓ Sorting will be the most emotional part of using *TOB*
- ✓ Sorting will take some thought and decision making
- ✓ Learn to say no when it comes to collecting everything you are offered or tempted to make your own possession
- ✓ Decide to release the emotional attachment to your things
- ✓ Consider what you really need to save for future use
- ✓ Determine to be unaffected by the status others assign to you

CHAPTER 7

SIDE 2: "SORT" THROUGH THE ITEMS

Now that you understand how to deal with the emotional aspect of sorting, it's time to learn how to sort. After all the items to be sorted from your space are in your box, you will need to have available the two bags clearly marked TRASH and GIVE AWAY. Then, find room to stretch out during sorting but not for your afternoon nap. This room is necessary to spread out the contents of your space as you remove them from your box. You might have to experiment a few times to see where you enjoy sorting the most.

You may wish to use a table top, countertop or grab a folding table and set it up for the sole purpose of sorting. One of my favorite places to sort is at our kitchen table. I have also used the kitchen countertops to sort. The point is to find a nice open place to sort the contents in your box. You may think, *Sure, Jackie, that sounds all fine and good; but what you can't see is that my table, countertops and every open place I could sort is too cluttered for me to sort the items in my box!* If that happens then you will want to clear off the table or the place you wish to sort in one fell swoop. Just clear it off. Even if you have to take everything off the table and put it on the floor, the point is to move it somewhere else. You will need a clear surface to sort and you won't want the items on the top of the table to distract you from sorting your box.

Since *TOB* can be used anywhere, you might decide that you want to sort in your car or at the park. You might wonder, where in the world would I find room to spread out the items to sort in those places? No problem at all! When I've sorted in my car, I've used the empty passenger seat and have spread out onto the dashboard. If you are at the park, look for a picnic table where you can place your piles. The point is that you will more than likely be able to find an area to spread your items out — just about anywhere. That's one of the many things I love about *TOB*. The versatility and practicality of it make decluttering so much easier than other ways you might have tried.

After you have a clear surface on which to sort your items, you will want to place the two bags marked TRASH and GIVE AWAY somewhere where you can access them as needed.

The way I begin sorting is to start with the first item I grab out of my box and place it somewhere on the table. It's best to not rummage around in the box looking for particular items to sort out. Just start with the items on top then work your way down even if you have to close your eyes and grab the first thing you feel.

After you grab the item, you will want to decide if it is trash or not. If the item is obviously trash like an empty wrapper, a pencil broken in half or a single staple, for example, then throw it away. If the item is not obviously trash, then place it on the table wherever you choose for similar items to be placed. As you continue pulling each item out of your box, trash it or place it on the table or wherever you are sorting with similar items. For example, you can make a pile that is used for writing utensils like pens, pencils, markers, crayons, etc.

Using the Halloween candy example again, my daughter chose to sort the candy by like candy. The lollipops in one pile, the gum in another pile, the Snickers in another pile and so on. You will want like items to be together. You may have to expand your sorting piles from the table to countertops or even the floor. Sometimes when I'm sorting and want to be in the same room as my family as they watch TV, I will grab my box then sort the items in piles around me on the floor. It's whatever works for you. Often when you get to the end of sorting, you will find that trash somehow manages to work itself to the bottom of your box. I like it when that happens because it certainly makes the ending part of clearing out the box easier.

After you grab that final item out of your box and sort it into its pile, you will have what seems like a thousand little piles lying on your table, the counter, the dashboard or maybe all over the floor. It will look like our table looked at Halloween after my daughter sorted her candy. Just getting to this point might be a challenge because you might not have ever categorized items together in this way before. It may seem strange to think of sorting things like this or actually sorting this way may make complete sense to you and will be easier to do than you thought. Either way, you will be happy because at that point your box will be finally empty.

The next part of sorting may evoke your emotions like we spoke of earlier. This part will be where you will go through each pile you have sorted and decide what items need to be left in the piles they are already in, which we will call the keep piles, or put into the give away bag or placed into the trash bag which you may have already used. The way I approach this part is to begin with the largest pile first and work my way around from the largest to smallest pile. I like to tackle the big stuff first because as I get closer to finishing, the little piles are less time consuming to sort through than the bigger ones. Sometimes I will approach the piles by choosing a corner pile and working through each pile in a row (I like making rows) until I have worked through all my piles. Really, it is whatever way works best for you.

Let's say that I have noticed the largest pile is where I have placed all the writing utensils. Remember, this pile contains a mixture of pens, pencils, crayons and markers. I decide to sort through the pens first to see exactly what all I have. After I look at the pile, I ask myself some questions about each pen and continue asking the same questions with the pencils then all other items in the pile. The questions I ask help me determine whether to keep, give away or trash each item. After you finish asking the questions, the only items left in the piles will be those items you chose to keep.

The first question I ask about the item is: "Is it broken?" If it is broken it goes into the trash. If you are debating on whether or not something is truly trash because you think that you might fix it someday, please don't entertain that thought for very long. Think of it this way, you haven't fixed it yet so the odds of it being fixed in the near future are slim. But if you are able to immediately fix it, then do it right now before you move on to the next item (like replacing batteries, taping something together). For example, during sorting I came across a battery operated pencil sharpener that was in good condition and I wanted to keep but it didn't work. It was no problem that two new AA batteries couldn't cure.

If the item is usable I ask myself the second question: "When did I last use this item?" This is where you need to put into perspective detaching from these items emotionally. If I haven't used the item in over a year it automatically goes into the give away bag. If you haven't used it in six months to one year, let it go. If it has tremendous emotional attachment, like the stone on my fireplace, but is something that I haven't "used" in a year and won't ever technically "use" it, I need to approach the item in a different way. With something like the stone from my ancestor's fireplace, I need to ask myself, "Is this something I could do without because I will choose to keep another item that belonged to my great—great grandfather?" Remember, the goal is to keep some—just not all.

Then I ask myself, "Do I have more than I really need of this item?" If so, then I need to be willing to let go and pass my blessing on to someone else. It's important to remember that there is always someone who can use something that you don't use anymore. Jesus wisely let us know that it is better to give than to receive. Your heart and home will be lighter when you give.

As I look at the item again, I question, "Will I use this item if I choose to keep it?" If I decide that I will not use a particular item or it doesn't make the cut to go with other items which will be saved for sentimental value, I have learned that it's okay to trash it.

Let's say you are sorting through your child's eighteen watercolor pictures from kindergarten. You realize that it is not necessary to keep all eighteen of them but you do want to keep some. This is where the answer to the final question of, "Can this item be one of a select few to go into a memory box?" would be a yes. (A memory box is what I call a special box where I like to store emotional items. It contains the things I want to keep for sentimental reasons. I have two under—the—bed boxes that I use as my memory boxes.) Having a memory box gives you a place to keep one or two of your child's paintings for yourself. You might also wish to place the paintings into plastic pages of a binder which will go into the memory box. Obviously you won't give away the rest of the paintings to the Salvation Army so it is okay to trash them. If you think Grandma or Grandpa would like a painting to keep, please make sure to contact them immediately to verify if they would like one or not. If so, place it in your giveaway bag and remember that the painting goes to Grandma.

As you move onto the next pile and go through each item there, ask yourself the same questions. At first, you might need to keep the list of questions close by in order to see what you are supposed to ask with each item. However, it won't take long before you won't have to consciously ask yourself the questions. You will eventually know what you are looking for with each item to determine if you will keep, give away or trash it.

So to help decide what to keep, give away or throw away, you will want to ask yourself these six questions:

Sorting Pile Questions:
1. Is this item broken or unusable?
2. When was the item last used?
3. Is this something I could do without because I will choose to keep another item instead?
4. Do I have more than I really need of this item?

5. Will I use this item if I choose to keep it?

6. Can this item be one of a select few to go into a memory box?

Once you have finished sorting, you will still have piles around you on the table, counter, dashboard or floor of the items you chose to keep. You will also have a bag of items to give away and a bag of trash. Here are some tips on what should be in the keep piles, the give away bag and the trash bag after you have finished sorting:

Keep Piles

These are items that you currently use or will use. You may choose to keep a few items from a pile if they have sentimental value and will be placed into a memory box.

Give Away Bag

These are items that have not been used in six months to a year yet could be usable or valuable to someone else. They are things you do not or will not use and are too nice to throw away.

When I organized my kids' toy box, I came across toys that my kids had outgrown and hadn't played with in a long time. The toys weren't broken so into the give away bag they landed for another child to enjoy.

Trash Bag

This is anything that is broken, is missing pieces or no one else would want. It is also anything that is plain old trash: wrappers, bits of paper, etc.

To go back to the example of sorting through my writing utensil pile, I continued to ask the questions for the remaining items in the pile. Taking the next pen from the pile that I thought I might like to keep, I asked myself "Is it broken or usable?"

The pen wasn't broken. After scribbling the pen on some scrap paper and only seeing a pressure indentation on the paper, I determined that the pen was not usable. Since no one would want a pen that doesn't work, into the trash bag it went.

As I grabbed the next pen, I saw that it was not broken. This time, as I scribbled it onto the paper I saw ink.

The next question I needed to answer was "When was this item last used?"

I didn't know the answer for this particular pen but on average, I knew that our household used pens quite frequently.

The next question was "Is this something I could do without

because I will choose to keep another item instead?"

The answer was no. I liked the way this pen wrote.

Asking the next question "Do I have more than I really need of this item?" I realized the short answer was, yes.

Then I asked "Will I use this item if I choose to keep it?"

In order to answer this question, I looked at the amount of writing utensils in my pile to sort through, and decided to keep 10 pens that worked. This would help ensure the item would be used. I chose to keep 10 pens since it was about one-third of the amount that was in my original pile to sort. Plus, I thought that number was a good amount to keep since I didn't know when this specific pen was last used. Figuring the four of us in our family could only write with one pen at a time, I reasoned that 10 pens should be enough.

It can sometimes be difficult to determine how much of a particular item you need to keep. You will figure it out over time but for now, base your estimate on how much you and your family currently use.

I ran into this problem with my towel closet. I knew that I wanted to scale down the number of towels due to the HUGE piles of laundry that were mostly towels. I figured the less towels we had to store the less laundry I would have.

It did mean that I would need to do laundry more often but I didn't mind since there were less towels taking up room in my linen closet. I decided to keep 12 towels out of the 30 we had. I figured 12 was a good amount since there were four of us. That meant if every day one towel was used then I would only have to wash towels (at the most) every three days. That was doable for me. I realized that getting rid of 18 towels (several of which ended up in the rag bin) was an amazing feeling AND I knew that ridding myself of all those towels would free up a lot of space in my linen closet. I also decided to keep two beach towels and five hand towels.

This was all based on my own family's need and how much extra I wanted to keep.

When it came to sheets, I decided since we have two twin beds and two full size beds that three sets of twin and full sheets were plenty for our needs. I reasoned that each bed could only have one sheet set on at a time, and I had one extra clean set when necessary. So now, when it is time to wash sheets, I wash both twin sets, and both full sets. This keeps me from procrastinating about laundry when I know we need the sheets or towels for that evening.

This process is also how I determined the amounts we would need from socks, spoons, shoes, pencils, jeans, dresses, pajamas and more. The most important thing you can do is to understand what you like and don't like. What works with your family? Are you willing to do what is necessary to maintain a lot of stuff or a little?

My advice is always that less is best. This is what makes the whole process of organizing such a great way to eliminate stress from your life.

The final question "Can this item be one of a select few to go into a memory box?" was easy to answer. I knew that this pen was not a memory item. It was used and needed frequently. So it went back onto the table in the pile to be kept.

As I continued sorting through my writing utensil pile, I grabbed the next pen. However, before I got a chance to ask myself the first of the 6 questions, I felt a tug at my heart as I looked at this particular pen. The pen evoked a strong memory deep within me. I realized the last two pens had been pretty easy to decide upon since I had no emotional connection. But, not this pen.

This pen had pictures of vintage Coca-Cola bottles all over it and the instant memory I received as I held it was when my son was in fifth grade. I had met him for lunch at school and had purchased the pen prior to lunch to give it to him as a little present. In fifth grade, pens were considered a luxury since the teachers only allowed their students to use pencils, so I knew he would like it. The memory was powerful for me and made me smile especially now that he was grown.

I began with the first question "Is it broken or unusable?" The pen did not look broken so I decided to see if it was usable. I scribbled and scribbled, yet couldn't get a single drop of ink to leak onto the paper. I really wanted this pen to work so I would have an excuse to keep it. *When sorting through items that evoke emotion, try to leave your emotional connection to the item checked out until you can see if it is usable.* No matter how much I scribbled, the pen wouldn't work.

I didn't know the answer to the next question of "When was the item last used?" because I didn't know how long ago the ink had dried up. I had a decision to make. Do I keep the pen for a memory or trash it? There was a twinge of guilt that wanted to creep up to make me feel as though I was getting rid of this wonderful memory if I trashed the pen. However, as I continued thinking about it, I knew there were many other items to remember my son's childhood by and this was one I was willing to let go of. I haven't missed it since. However, if I decided the pen was a memory item that I wanted to keep, it would not have gone back into the pen keep pile. I would have put it aside to go into my memory box.

Earlier, we talked about what a memory box is. Now, I'd like to share an example of how much should be placed into a memory box. In my basement, whole boxes of sentimental items were in the form of my children's baby clothes, toys and such. Since these items were already in a box, I didn't need to place them into my box. When I was ready to sort through these five boxes, I nervously dug in. As I opened each box of baby items, I realized I had a conundrum on my hands. Opening the first box smacked a tidal wave of emotion right across my heart. When opening a box of strong emotions like these boxes, there is a great temptation to snuggle in as you go through each item remembering happy and/or sad memories with each item.

Sorting is not time to take a stroll down memory lane. Sorting is a time for decluttering and deciding (with focused intention) on what you need as well as what you do not need. This is important to understand and agree upon with yourself from the outset. Know that there will be some items which you will encounter that are going to create a desire to sit with them and walk down the past. Resist this urge. It is ok to remember but as much as is possible stay in the here and now as you work through these items. You are looking to keep the things that are necessary for you now.

As I lifted the first tiny outfit out of the box I decided to look at it as objectively as possible.

Cute little outfit that my son wore, I thought.

Next, another cute little outfit that my son wore. How many of these were there?

As I thought about it logically I acknowledged that we were not planning to have any more children so to keep these outfits for a future child of mine was impractical. Besides there was someone somewhere who could use these outfits and enjoy them as much as I did. Some of the outfits that I had kept actually shocked me because a lot of them were not able to be used by someone else due to broken snaps, nasty spit up stains and other things on them. That was when I decided to think about why I wanted to keep these outfits, toys, shoes and such.

I wanted to be able to look back and remember those days if I chose to. So I decided that I would keep a few things. I decided to keep the outfits that each of our kids wore home from the hospital after they were born. I also kept my favorite outfits and shoes from their baby days. I kept a couple of crocheted blankets my grandmother made. I kept one toy from each child. I kept each one's "Baby's First Year Calendar" that had a lock of their hair and other great memories like when they rolled over for the first time. This was more than enough to fulfill any future desires to stroll down memory lane when I was NOT in the process of cleaning out.

As I placed the other items in the give away bag, I was reminded by one particular outfit of something that made the choice to give away most of these things much easier. I absolutely loved this little jean skirt and purple onesie but I remembered that a friend had given it to me when my daughter was first born. In fact, this friend had given me several bags full of baby girl clothes. She asked me to use the clothes then continue to pass them on to someone else.

At that moment of sorting through those items, I was inspired by her generosity and kindness. Why would I be hesitant to give away something I didn't need especially since she was so generous to give to me from her memories? This made the process much easier. Remember, there is always someone who can use something that you do not.

Finally, there were just a few items left from my kids' baby days that I had left out to keep and the rest were in the give away bag. These items then made their way into my memory box which I can go through whenever I want to take a stroll down memory lane and laugh or cry. However, now I have the satisfaction of knowing my five big boxes that were full of baby items and clothes were condensed then placed into the memory box. I kept some but not all.

After you have finished sorting your last pile you will probably feel very enthusiastic. Clearing out all the extra items that previously had taken up so much room along with seeing the items you wish to keep in piles will bring peace and relief.

Sorting through your box will take a while especially the very first time you sort. After time, sorting will be something that you won't even have to think about and it will become easier.

It's important to note what to do with the give away and trash bags. If the bags are full or too heavy to pick up, then you will want to get rid of them. If it's trash, obviously throw it away. If it's to be given away, then you will want to take it to a local charity as soon as possible. Often, these places will come and pick up your donations at your home. You might want to call the place you wish to donate and ask to schedule a pick up day or put the bag in your trunk. The next time you are running errands, drop it off at your local charity.

The important thing is to get them out of your home ASAP.

CHAPTER 7 SUMMARY

✓ Find a place to sort through your box

✓ Place labeled Trash Bag and Give Away Bag close by as you sort

✓ Go through each item in your box to sort by like items and place into piles

✓ Go through each pile looking for items to keep, give away or trash

✓ Ask questions about each item:

1. Is it broken or useable?

2. When was this item last used?

3. Is this something I could do without because I will choose to keep another item instead?

4. Do I have more than I really need of this item?

5. Will I use this item if I choose to keep it?

6. Can this item be one of a select few to go into a memory box?

✓ "Keep" items are items you use or will use

✓ "Give away" items have not been used within six months to a year and could be valuable to someone else

✓ "Trash" is anything broken or that no one else would want

✓ A memory box is a great way to keep a few items you don't use but don't want to get rid of either

✓ The goal is to keep some but not all

CHAPTER 8

SIDE 3: "ASSIGN" A HOME FOR YOUR ITEMS

When I was a little girl, one of my favorite things to do was visit my mother's cousin, Nina, and her husband, Don. They lived about 20 minutes from our home and we visited them a couple times a year. At that time, Nina and Don didn't have children so they always made over me whenever we visited. However, that wasn't the main reason why I liked visiting them, although it is always fun to be made over when you are a child. You see, Nina had once shown me a cabinet in her living room where she kept several coloring books along with one of those 64 count crayon boxes with the sharpener in the back of the box. As she showed me the stash, she gave me permission to open the cupboard to use the crayons and books whenever I wanted.

For some reason, getting those crayons and books out was the main thing I looked forward to whenever my mom announced we would be visiting Nina. I don't know if it was the fact that I could go into someone else's home, open up her cupboard and remove something to use without asking for permission, or if it was the fact that I could color with brand new, pointy crayons and could sharpen them as often as I wanted with the cool little sharpener. My crayons at home were broken, worn down and didn't have the sharpener. It probably was a combination of the two things but whatever the reason, I remember making a beeline straight for the crayon cupboard after we walked into Nina's home and said hello. Then, when it was time to go home or I had finished creating a masterpiece for Nina to hang on her refrigerator, I would close up the box, gather the coloring books together and walk back to the cupboard. I would place them back in their home and close the door, knowing that my colorful friends would be waiting for me the next time I visited.

When things in our home have a place to live or a place where they are assigned to be then it is easy to find what we are looking for. We know right where to look for them. If the scissors live in or are assigned to be placed in the top, right drawer in the kitchen, then whenever someone needs scissors, they know where to go to get them. This "assigning" a home to our items creates a peace within the home. There is a consistency in knowing that a particular item can be found in the same place every time. Assigning a home to each item also is a great time saver.

I can remember before I assigned a home to my scissors, when I actually needed to use the scissors, I sometimes spent a half hour or so looking for them. If I did find them, I was so worked up and stressed out over the time I had wasted looking for them, that any peace I had been experiencing vanished. It was replaced with irritation, frustration and anger. Each minute is so valuable. Time spent looking unnecessarily for minor things like scissors was enough to raise my blood pressure and my temper.

So now that you have *gathered* together the items in your box from the space you have chosen to declutter and have *sorted* through each pile, item by item, deciding what to keep, give away or throw away, it's now time to *assign* a home or a place for the keep pile items to live.

Most of the sorted items you have sitting on your table (or wherever you have sorted) will be assigned back into the space left. However, many items will not return there. This is the time to decide how you would like to use the space that is now empty. What do you think should be assigned to live there? To answer this, you must determine what makes the most sense for the space to hold. Decide based on its location. Bathrooms don't need to have toys in them unless they are "bath" toys.

For example, when I first organized my junk drawer in the kitchen, it was difficult for me to determine what items I wanted to assign to this drawer since there was such an eclectic mixture of items that had come out of it. To help me decide, I looked at the location of the drawer and the drawer's functionality. The junk drawer itself was the bottom, corner drawer in the kitchen directly next to the kitchen table. The kitchen table was where the kids worked on homework, where papers were colored or art drawn and it was kind of like an extended workspace when we were not eating. The drawer was also the biggest drawer in the kitchen, as far as height goes, which is why it made such a great junk drawer because so much could fit into it. Since this had been a junk drawer, it made the decision a bit more difficult because there was such a mixture of what seemed to be a little bit of everything; pens, rubber bands, staples, toys, papers, maps, batteries, stickers and much more. I looked at the first pile sitting on the table that I had completely sorted. It was all the pens, pencils and markers I had chosen to keep. As I continued to look at the piles I realized that most of the items that came from the drawer seemed to be basic office supplies. I decided that this drawer would be a great place to assign the pens, pencils, staplers, notecards, rulers, scissors and all the basic office supplies since we used these items at the table most of the time. As I looked at the sorted items spread out across that same table, I realized that most of these things would be going back into the drawer. However, some of them would *not* be going back to that particular space. I didn't let that distract me. Deciding to work with the items in piles on the table that I would assign to the drawer first, I went to work.

The function of the junk drawer had changed. No longer would it collect everything, like a junk drawer does, but now all the office supply items would live there. This made the decision of what would go back into that space much easier.

As my eyes scanned the piles on the table, I chose to start with the pens, pencils and markers. The problem I now had was *how* would they go back into the drawer? When I had originally gathered them from the drawer and put them into my box, they were scattered all throughout the drawer in a willy-nilly, haphazard way. I knew they needed to be put back neatly and orderly; I just wasn't certain *how* to accomplish that.

Several options crossed my mind on how to keep them neatly together. I thought that I could wrap a rubber band around all the pens, another around the pencils and yet another around the markers. However, that didn't seem to be the best option for me or my family. I knew the odds that my family and I would put a pen back into a rubber banded group would be slim. It is a little difficult to squeeze a pen back into a banded pile again. That would mean that I would be right back where I started with a drawer full of items carelessly strewn throughout.

Keep this in mind as you are considering how to organize the items. What will be the easiest way for you and your family to continue keeping the space uncluttered and neat in the future? I figured if I could somehow keep the pens and pencils together in a type of container, in the drawer, it was highly probable that our family would be able to put a pen or pencil back. But where could I get that container? I didn't want to go out and purchase some type of container, although that would work.

In order to keep on task and to make the best use of time, I would recommend making a list of the things you would like to pick up at the store to help make the space orderly. Then place the piles of items in the drawer neatly. After you have had a chance to make it to the store later in the day or at the most, a day or two later, you can place the contents of the drawer into the new containers.

I decided to get creative and look around the house for things I didn't need that could be used to help keep my organized items together.

I had a cylinder container that was currently holding hot chocolate mix in the kitchen. I thought that it would be perfect as a pen/pencil container and since my drawer was tall enough, the container would fit. So, I grabbed the hot chocolate mix container, which was half full, took a storage baggie out of the cupboard and dumped the mix into the storage bag. After placing the bag of mix back into the cupboard (where that bag would eventually go was not my concern right then), I wiped out the inside of the container and placed all the pens and pencils inside it. They fit perfectly. I even had room for something else. As I looked around at the piles on the table I spotted the scissors. I realized that those would fit perfectly in the container and they would be easy to reach with the handle facing up.

Next, I moved on to the pile of rubber bands. In my pile of rubber bands, there was the original bag the bands came in along with many loose ones. How did I want to place the rubber bands back into their assigned drawer? I figured I could put them all into the original bag but scrapped that idea since the bag only had a tiny hole to pull them through and if I made the hole bigger, the bag would be ruined. I thought of two options. Put all of the rubber bands into a baggie, which could be sealed, or make a rubber band ball. I'm sure there were other options; those were just the two that I came up with at that time. Now, if my children had been around at that moment and were looking for something to do, I may have chosen the rubber band ball idea and let one of them do that. Instead, I chose the baggie. The baggie seemed a quick and easy fix plus I had plenty of baggies in the cupboard.

You have probably noticed that I tend to use things that are already in my home as containers to hold items (hot chocolate box, baggies, etc.). This approach is helpful for me in two ways. First, I am able to keep my items neatly together in containers that I have specifically designed or marked out for a particular use. Second, by using boxes, baggies, containers or cans that are lying around the house, I have eliminated clutter from other places in my home and used it creatively in a different spot. However, there are plenty of stores where you can purchase bins, baskets and containers if you wish to do so. There are many fine products that will suit the needs of your particular drawer, shelf or cupboard; you just need to know the purpose of the drawer, shelf or cupboard and what items you will assign to live there.

You probably have a basket lying around, or a box of hot cocoa that has at least one packet left in it. Use it. Just take the packets out, cut the top flaps off the box, and voila, you have a place to store your pencils. You can even take some tape along with the top flaps you cut off and use them to make a divider in the middle of the cocoa box. This way, you can keep your pens and scissors on the side opposite the pencils. You will be amazed at the things you already own in your home that can double as an inexpensive organizer.

For now, I had a cylinder container full of my pens, pencils and scissors which was assigned to the drawer along with a baggie full of rubber bands. Looking at the piles on the table that would be assigned to the drawer I realized that I would like to use a type of basket or small, short-sided box to contain the loose items that could not be grouped together. I also thought I could place the bag of rubber bands in the container to keep the baggie from sliding around the bottom of the drawer. After a quick trip to the local dollar store, I found a long, flat bottom basket that was perfect. I came home, placed the stapler, staples, the baggie of rubber bands, a baggie of pencil top erasers, rulers, a compass, sticky notes, a baggie of paper clips and a few other things into the basket that would now be assigned to this drawer. Then I took the other containers, placed them into the drawer and arranged them in a way that I liked. Looking down at the drawer and its contents, I felt a relief and tremendous pride in the work I had just accomplished in gathering, sorting then assigning all the items from this space. Finally, I had another spot that was organized. My family and I now knew where to find the items assigned there.

As you are assigning, understand that some spaces will be easier to assign items to than others. For example, when I decluttered my piano bench, it was pretty easy for me to assign the items that would live there. Obviously, music books, some music staff paper, a pencil and music flashcards would live in that space. The tricky part of the assignment lay in deciding what music books to assign there. I owned more music books than could possibly fit. For the most part, the piano bench itself made the task of assigning easier since the bench served a particular purpose. I placed the top few books that I played from the most in it.

Other places, like the junk drawer we talked about earlier, were a little more difficult to assign since it could hold just about anything I wanted it to. The best way to decide what to assign to a space is to look at what is currently there. Look for the type of items it collects. This will be a good indicator of what items should be assigned to it.

Now that my items assigned to the drawer were neatly in place, I looked at what was left on the table. There were actually quite a few piles of items left over. A question of panic hit me, "What in the world do I do with all the things in these piles?"

As I looked over each pile, a pleasant thought countered the panic thought. "Well, at least all of the items left in these piles are things I use and want to keep." Since I didn't know what to do with these items, I thought of two options. I could put these items in another box, put the box somewhere and get to it later. I didn't care for that option since it seemed to be creating another box to go through. However, this option might work for you.

The second option I liked better was to put the sorted items in another space in my home where they would best fit. For example, there were crayons and stickers left on the table. I knew that I wanted these to go to somewhere where craft supplies would be assigned. Since I didn't have that place just yet, I decided to put the crayons where I remembered seeing some other crafty things and that was in the hall closet on a shelf. Even though the closet wasn't decluttered yet, it was still ok for me to place these items there because eventually I would be getting to that closet. When I did, the crayons and stickers would be waiting for me.

As you finish your sorting, take each pile left on your table and place every item from the pile in other places of your home.

After you have put away the last pile, it is time to celebrate. You did it. Sit back and relax. You have done a great thing and you deserve to just bask in the moment. Gaze at your work. Admire how great it looks. The process you have undertaken to get to this point has definitely been labor intensive in mind and body, but you are now able to witness and enjoy the fruit of your labors. You have worked hard to get to this point, so it is time to show off how you have organized space number one. Find someone or even your entire family or friends to show it to and let them enjoy the beauty with you. Also, let them know that you would like their help in order to keep it looking as great as it does now. We will discuss in detail in the following chapter how to enlist your family or those living with you in helping you maintain the order. Just make sure you show it off, and be proud.

I would like to take a minute here to tell you about my friend Tammy, and how we worked through the three steps of *TOB* that we have talked about.

When Tammy asked for my assistance with her home and I paid her a visit, she welcomed and offered me a seat at the dining room table. As I sat down, she pushed everything that was scattered across the table to the other side, leaving a half cleared table top where we sat. Tammy apologized for the mess, pulled out a chair, moved a sweater off the chair, placed it onto another chair and sat down. I asked Tammy what space she would first like to organize in her home. She began to list several, such as the kitchen and the living room. She told me that she and her family use these rooms the most often. As we talked, her young son walked to where we were sitting, pulled out a chair and sat down. He placed his toys on top of the clutter that covered half the table and began to play. When Tammy finished I asked, "How often do you use this table?"

"Every day," she answered.

"What do you use it for?"

"Well, when anyone comes over, this is where we sit. We eat our meals here, do homework here, talk here, actually we do most things here at the table."

I was curious, "When you eat meals here at the table, what do you do with the things that are on the table?"

Tammy dropped her eyes and confessed, "I push everything to one end of the table and we eat at the other end."

I realized that Tammy's table had become a catch-all and saw that the table would be a great place for her to start with her box. Like most of us, Tammy had become so used to the disorder in her home that she failed to see the forest for the trees.

I told Tammy that while the kitchen and living room seemed like great places to begin, it would actually be better to consider starting with a smaller space where she would see almost immediate results. Some place where she would not have to wait weeks to see success. "Someplace like this," I suggested, pointing to the dining room table.

"The table?" Tammy raised her eyebrows.

"Think about it. This table was where you brought me to sit. It's the place where your family seems to spend a lot of time and it's one of the first things someone notices when they walk into your home."

It took her a moment to let the thought sink in. She had never considered the table as a place that you would organize. After all, it was a table, not a drawer, closet or room.

She looked at the table, looked back at me and said, "I love it! Let's do it."

When Tammy said she was ready, that meant that she needed to follow the steps that you and I have talked about so far in using *TOB*: **Gathering, Sorting** *and* **Assigning**. Once the items on the table were completely cleared off (along with the stuff on the chairs) and placed into Tammy's box, we cleaned the table top. We wiped it down, sprayed some polish on it and pushed the chairs in. As we looked for somewhere to sort through her box, I knew we didn't want to use the table top to sort. That would be putting the items right back onto the table. So we improvised and used other surfaces to sort in order to keep the table clear. It's always ok to find a corner of the floor and start pulling things out of your box right there. You can sort on the floor as long as you are out of the pathway of anyone in your house.

Tammy and I flew through sorting since there were not a lot of items and most of the items were big.

After the items were sorted, it was time to assign the items that would go back onto the table. I asked Tammy what she would like to assign to the table meaning what items she would like to keep on her table. She struggled a bit with the answer, not really knowing what to say.

Often, the decision of assigning items to particular spaces can be overwhelming. We are not used to viewing our home as little spaces within a bigger one. This is where Tammy struggled. To think of each item as assigned to a particular space meant she must think about individual small spaces within her home instead of larger spaces such as the bedroom, bathrooms, living rooms, etc. Instead, we more or less see our home as the place where we and *everything* in it lives. Thinking in this new way takes some getting used to. To get your thoughts moving in this direction try to picture how the particular space you are organizing (in this case, a dining room table) would look in a magazine if it were featured in a beautiful, professional photo in that magazine. Perhaps it would have a vase of flowers in the middle or maybe flowers and a big bowl of fruit. Can you see it with placemats and a candle as a centerpiece? Or if your magazine is minimalist, the table may have nothing on it, completely empty. In order to picture the space most clearly, think of its function. Think of how the space will be used the most. Think of its location in your home. Think of the easiest way to keep it neat.

I asked Tammy how she envisioned her table and discovered that she pictured her family sitting at the table using napkins, along with salt and pepper from off the table. She pictured a pretty basket with the napkins and shakers in the center of the table. Picturing her space this way was how we determined what items from our sorted piles would go back onto the table. The only items going back onto the table were napkins and the salt/pepper shakers. We took the other items that had been sorted belonging to Tammy's son into his room. The items that belonged in the kitchen, went into the kitchen. We didn't worry about where in her son's room or where in the kitchen the items would go because for us the focus was on the table, nowhere else for the moment. We placed the kitchen items on the kitchen counter with all the other items already there. And we placed her son's items on the dresser in his room.

After placing all the other sorted items somewhere else in the house, we were left with just the napkins and the salt/pepper shakers. We placed the salt/pepper shakers and the napkins in the center of the table. However, we were missing one thing, the pretty little basket where Tammy had pictured placing the napkins and salt/pepper shakers. So we went on a treasure hunt. Instead of heading to the store and purchasing a basket to bring home, we decided it was best to check around her home first. Since Tammy had envisioned a basket on her table, more than likely, the odds were great that Tammy already uses baskets to store or decorate in her home. I told her we might be able to find just the basket she had envisioned somewhere in her home. After looking around for a little bit, Tammy announced that she had found the perfect basket. Of course, the basket was filled to the brim with clutter but it was the perfect fit for the table. She removed the items from the basket, wiped it out and placed it in the center of the table. She arranged the napkins along with the salt/pepper shakers in the basket and we both stepped back to admire the reality of Tammy's mental magazine picture. In a couple of hours, her dining room table had gone from cluttered to open, clear and pretty. Seeing this made it easy to celebrate Tammy's success.

Now that you are finished assigning, like Tammy, you have one space in your home that is neat and orderly. It's where everything has a place and everything is in its assigned place. Remember, if you previously made a list of containers to purchase for your first project, you will want to get to the store as soon as possible.

This is an inspiring moment as you realize that you have organized your first space with *TOB* and you are capable of finishing the rest of your home. However, the process is not over completely. In fact, I feel the next part of maintaining is the most important part of the whole process. Keeping your space orderly will ensure that you will be able to continue reaping the rewards of your triumph. But for right now, enjoy the success of a job most wonderfully done.

CHAPTER 8 SUMMARY

- ✓ Decide what items to assign to live in the organized space based on where it is located and what makes the most sense for it to hold
- ✓ Contain your piles in baggies, baskets or however you choose in order to fit their newly assigned "home"
- ✓ Place the items into their newly assigned space and make a list of containers or organizer items you may wish to purchase

✓ For the piles left on the table that are unassigned to this particular space, put the items into other places where they would somewhat fit

✓ If necessary, purchase baskets or create containers as soon as possible to help keep your piles within the new space orderly

CHAPTER 9

SIDE 4: "MAINTAIN" THE ORGANIZATION

I once heard of a woman who had lost 100 pounds through hard work, determination and self-control. Her friends and family celebrated the tremendous milestone with congratulations saying, "How did you do it?" and "I could never do that!"

However, after the excitement waned and life settled back into life, the excitement of her new body began to fade as it become familiar to her. Months later she saw a friend she had not seen in some time. The friend commented on the weight loss and asked how difficult it had been to lose that much weight. The woman answered, "It wasn't easy to lose the weight but I think it was easier to lose the weight than to continue to keep it off."

I think everyone who has overcome any type of personal struggle whether it is losing weight, training for a marathon or quitting smoking, knows that the difficult part lies in continuing the victory over the battle that was fought and won. Maintaining anything takes fortitude and tenacity but the key to the continued victory is to make a conscious effort to keep on keeping on. Once victory is claimed over anything hard fought over, it is most important to make sure that one does not settle back into old ways and old habits. Let the new habits that are formed in approaching this new way of living be your guide.

It has been said that we can remove a negative thought from our mind but in order for it to continue to stay away we must replace it with a positive thought. We must create new positive thoughts and then choose those thoughts daily. Over time, the positive thoughts will push away the negative and a new way of thinking will begin to take hold. Eventually, this positive way of thinking will become automatic in our brains.

The same is true with organizing. It's one thing to initially clear clutter with *TOB*; however, it's a completely different thing to stay that way. Once a space has become neat, it will quickly go back to its original messy state if the order is not maintained. This last step is one that will continue long after the initial decluttering has occurred with *TOB*.

After you have organized the first space in your home, my recommendation would be to wait two weeks before you attempt to move on to the next one. After you see your first results, it will be tempting to tackle more drawers, cupboards or shelves but please hesitate before doing so. Use the two weeks to work on the final step of maintaining what you just organized.

This doesn't mean that to be successful with future areas in your home you will have to wait two weeks after you organize a space. Just wait that long the very first time. However, you may feel the need to wait two weeks after the second or third space, also. Be sure to wait as long as necessary to make the neatness a habit for you and your family.

So what do you do during those two weeks? One thing you want to ensure is that everyone in your home has seen the new tidy space. This should have happened when you completed the assigning part in the last chapter. If you didn't show off your space then, now is certainly the time to do so. The other thing to do is to place items back into their exact assigned space when finished using them.

After you have completed that first space, if you need a particular item from there, you will be able to go right to it. Then, as soon as you are finished using it, the item needs to be put back into the same place from where it came. At first, putting things back where they live may seem annoying, but it will become a habit after you get used to doing it.

However, getting your family to cooperate with you in putting items back where they are assigned after they have used them might be even more challenging. Be encouraged, because the same process you used to train yourself is the same process that you can share with your family. Help them understand they need to put things back when they are finished with them to continue keeping that spot neat.

What can you reasonably expect from others in helping with this? After all, aren't they partly to blame for all the work you had to do to declutter? Perhaps they helped contribute to the mess you used to have in your newly organized spot. But so have you. So it's time to practice what you preach. Show them how by putting things back when you are finished using them yourself. Put things back from where they came. In other words, leave it where you found it. Let them know that this does not apply if they found something lying on the floor that belongs somewhere specific.

This was a tremendous help for me after I had cleared out the piano bench. I called the family together and showed them the efforts of my hard work. You might get a roll of the eyes when you do this, but make sure to do it regardless of how they respond. It's important for your family to see the results of your work and then to know what items will be assigned to the space. They will also know what does NOT go there.

I showed my family the completed project of the piano bench. I told them that the piano bench was no longer a place to hide trash, excess papers or anything else except music, three pencils and sticky notes. Letting them know what items belonged there encouraged me since I had empowered them to help keep the bench neat. I felt I didn't have to do it alone, nor would I have to. Does this mean that I never found anything in the piano bench besides the items that belong there? No. Does this mean that I never found a piece of music laying around on the steps or on the living room floor? Of course not! That would mean we are an absolutely perfect family which is definitely not the case. What it does mean is that I am not solely responsible for maintaining all the organization in my home. It is a shared home and a shared responsibility. There are some members of my family who tend to put things back almost on auto—pilot and there are some members who have to be asked, "Is this where the scissors go?" To which they answer a reluctant, "No." Then they are asked to please put the scissors where they belong. This is very important and cannot be overstated in any way. It is not up to you to be chasing after everyone, picking up the things they have left scattered across your home and placing them back where they belong. Enlist and expect this of those with whom you live. It will make this final side of *TOB* much easier.

Realistically, you will find things thrown around that belong in a certain space. Am I saying that you should never put anything away unless you get it out yourself? Absolutely not! Helping your family by putting some things away that they may have gotten out is also helping you get into the habit. But you want to teach your family the importance of respecting those who live with you by putting things where they belong. Help them a little if needed but don't pick up after them all the time.

As I said before, you cannot expect your family to help you stay organized if you are not willing to do it yourself. This is sometimes a difficult habit to get into.

Don't forget that you are helping those who live with you. You are helping them learn how to maintain their neat living space.

Hopefully, they will carry the practice with them wherever they go.

Remember Tammy from the last chapter? As we sat down at what seemed like a new dining room table, we celebrated the beauty and peace of the tidy space. However, after a few moments we began to talk about how she could keep the table looking the way it did at that moment. I explained to Tammy that she needed to share the new table with her family and how she could keep it orderly.

First, *everyone in the home needs to understand the function of the space and what is assigned there.*

In order for Tammy to successfully obtain help from those who share her home, she had to take the first step to make certain everyone in her family understood the function of the newly cleared and organized table. They needed to know what items were now assigned to that space. Tammy would have to relay to each member of her family what function the table would serve. The table would still function as the hub of activity and gathering. The difference would now be that the only items that would stay on the table were the items assigned to the table. The napkins and shakers in the basket would be the only items assigned to stay on the table top.

Before leaving, I told Tammy that her homework would be to gather her family together and show them how the table looked now.

Second, *train yourself to put things back from where they came.*

It was important that Tammy began to get into the habit of putting things back where they belonged when she left the table. For example, let's say a friend stops by to visit Tammy. They sit at the table for coffee and dessert. After the friend leaves, Tammy needs to remove all the items that are not assigned or belong on the table (which in this case would be the items she placed on the table during her friend's visit). Then after the table is cleared off, the only thing left sitting on the table would be the napkins and shakers in the basket. Tidying up like this includes any crumbs left on the table. The best way for Tammy to keep the table orderly, when finished using it, would be to clear away any items she brought to the table, wipe the table if necessary and push the chairs back in. Tammy needed to get into the habit of leaving neat spaces the way she found them.

As we discussed maintaining, Tammy mentioned an issue that seemed counterproductive to her success. "What should I do when, I am working on something at the table and then realize, for example, it's time to pick up my son from school? I know that when I come home, I will want to continue working on the project at the table. Should I clean it up and clear it away from the table every time I leave the house?"

It was a great question and I liked how she was thinking ahead.

"Tammy, anytime you leave the table to do something else, I would suggest that you establish the habit of putting away any items you have brought to the table from somewhere else. Even though you have every intention to resume your project when you return from picking up your son, there might be something else that needs your attention. You might not be able to get back to that project until another day. When you sit down to the table for dinner, you are left with a messy table, the opposite of what you are trying to achieve."

Tammy looked away, "That is true. After school, I usually talk with him about his day. The rest of the evening seems to be busy with family things. I probably wouldn't get back to the project till possibly the next day. But, it would normally stay on the table throughout dinner and be waiting for me the next day."

Develop the habit of putting items back where you found them (ideally in the assigned space where they live). I developed this habit by ensuring all items were placed back where they were assigned and that the space looked neat before I left the house or went to bed. This might take an extra minute or two and might seem obsessive compulsive at first but believe me when I say that once it becomes a habit, you will do it without even thinking. The results will be the motivation to keep up the habit. You don't have to go through your entire house or open every drawer. Just a quick scan will alert you if a spot needs attention. After being away from home, peace and rest will meet you at the door when you open it. You will be glad to come home.

This is a great habit to get into before you go to bed each night. There is nothing like waking up in the morning and walking into a kitchen, bathroom or living room that is orderly. It produces a calming, relaxing environment that is the incentive to keep it up. For example, let's say you have organized your junk drawer. If you leave it the way you found it (by putting things back where they are assigned whenever you open that drawer) a beautiful picture of neatness and order will greet your eyes. You can easily see and know everything that is in the drawer.

In addition to putting items from the table back where they

belonged, I challenged Tammy to develop the habit of scanning and clearing. For the next two weeks, she needed to scan the table several times throughout the day and prior to bedtime, to make sure it was cleared off. When no one was using the table, she needed to see that the chairs were pushed in and crumbs removed. Scanning and clearing before bed ensured Tammy that each morning, when she came into the dining room; she was pleasantly greeted "Good morning!" from her beautifully clear table. Order and peace would set the mood for the entire day.

Third, *enlist the help of your family or those who live with you to put things back. Thank them when they do.*

Remember, when you showed your family the results of your hard work? You explained to them what the function of the space will be and asked for their help. This is good for them.

The ability to create and maintain organization is a gift that we can give to our children. A gift that will benefit them for a lifetime. It will bring order to their personal, academic and professional life. Let me offer you this encouragement, just as it will become a habit for us if we consistently put things back to their assigned place, this new way will also become a habit for your kids. Really, it will. My family is living proof of that. In the drawer I described earlier, the scissors were assigned and lived in that drawer. Over the course of several years, my now teen daughter, began to put the scissors back where they were assigned, most of the time. In fact, if she opens the drawer now to use the scissors and doesn't see them, she will ask someone where the scissors are. She knows that drawer is where the scissors always belong.

When we become used to something residing in a particular place for a while and then it happens to not be there, it seems very odd to us.

Think of someplace in your neighborhood that has a tree. You might have to really think about it because we are so used to seeing trees around us that we don't notice them. Now imagine if that tree blew down in a windstorm and the trunk, branches and stump are hauled away. There is no trace or evidence that a tree existed in that place. In your mind, something would be missing, you might not be able to put your finger on it at first but you would know that something was different. It would stand out. That is how it will be once you begin using *TOB*. The first thing that will stand out most is the neat space but then after a while you will come to expect to see it neat. When an item is out of place, like the scissors, it will be obvious. The family and those living with you will want to know what is going on. Don't give up, you are teaching and learning valuable lessons together. When they do put things back where they live, compliment them. Tell them how much you appreciate their help and effort in maintaining the order. Tell them how much it means to you that they appreciate the hard work you put into creating an organized spot.

Fourth, *when you want to purchase or accept something, first determine if you really need it.*

In order to maintain, you need to keep purchasing and your acceptance of given items in check. There is a reason we got to the point where chaos and disorder have ruled much of our lives. In Chapter Six, we discussed how easy it is to accumulate possessions and how it can become very difficult to rid ourselves emotionally of their hold. The best way to keep from accumulating items we don't need is to be aware of what we really need when we are shopping, whether it is a yard sale or if someone offers to give us something. You have worked very hard to get your space orderly. When you are at a store or a yard sale and are thinking about making a purchase, stop. Ask yourself the following questions:

1. Do I have this item or something similar to this at home?

2. Instead of purchasing or taking this item, do I know someone or someplace that has a similar item that I can borrow to use and then return when I am finished?

3. Is this an emotional purchase or an emotional acceptance of something free?

4. Do I really need this item? If yes, why?

Often, our purchases are emotional ones that we later realize we didn't really need but were caught up in the moment. If you do decide to purchase the item or accept it from someone, before it even makes it inside your door, decide where it will live. In fact, picture the new item in the space where you will assign it. Will it fit? Will you have to make any changes to the space you plan to assign it?

Once you bring it home, immediately put it in its assigned space. This will save you the problem of the new item cluttering your home until you find a place for it. Practice saying, "No thank you," when someone offers to give you something that you don't really need.

Fifth, *when something new comes in, something old goes out.*

To help maintain your organized space, it's best to think of something you can give or throw away when you bring a new item into your home. This was a difficult concept for me to follow through with when I started with *TOB*.

Obviously, you will continue to purchase items and will be given items from generous friends. The problem lies in the way those items begin to creep up on you. If you never give or throw away anything after you first use *TOB*, you will end up with a houseful of clutter again.

When we talked about our possessions in Chapter Six, we discussed how important it is to be able to let go of things easily. I once heard someone say that when we receive gifts from Heaven our palms are turned up to receive them. Instead of holding tightly onto those things, we need to hold them loosely and be willing to release to someone else if need be. It is best to live with our possessions in open hands. Always be ready to let go when it's time.

In James, we are told that every good gift is from above, coming down from our heavenly Father. All that has been given to us is a gift from God. We need to be ready to release any gift He has given us when we need to. When we live our lives as channels of giving, we truly experience lasting joy and peace. Living like this is the best way to guard against major clutter issues in the future.

You will find as you continue to release things that you will become more content. Live with a thankful heart. Be grateful for the things you have been given and be happy when you can pass those things on to someone else to enjoy.

As I worked through our spaces, I realized that we had an issue with books. We love books and it seemed that we all collected them. When a book made its residence within our home, it never left. While at first I thought this was a good thing, I soon realized that only so many books fit on each bookshelf. So, of course, they began to spill out onto the floor, into the closet and really wherever they ended up getting shoved. The thought of giving away *any* book made me feel sick. I loved the smell, the memories and the stories from these books. In fact, twice a year, our local library has its semi—annual book sale. Our family has always enjoyed the book sales. It was especially fun when our children were young. Going through boxes and boxes of books just looking for the next ones that would fill their little bookcase in their rooms was a treat for them.

After wrestling with the emotional connection I had to books, I realized that even if I gave away some books, there were plenty of libraries around our area where we could borrow those same titles if we wanted to read them again. So, in order to make room for new books, prior to each book sale, the kids and I went through our collection of books on our shelves. We looked for books already read and many re-read that we could give to the sale where someone else could purchase them. The money going to the library and the books going into someone else's home to enjoy was a great thing to remember as we chose what books we would release. I told the kids that we would only keep the amount of books that would fit on our bookshelves. In addition, for each book we bought new or used, we would get rid of the same number of books from our own shelf.

Over the years, this one habit of giving away as many books as we purchase has been a tremendous help in keeping our home free of looking like it is a used bookstore. For the record, we have never had a shortage of books. Of course, we keep our absolute favorite titles with dog-eared pages and broken bindings but the majority of books have come and gone through the years. We also have the satisfaction of knowing that we have contributed to helping fund local libraries and have let many good books pass through our hands to others. This same thought can be applied to clothes, board games, toys, dishes, etc. When something new comes into my home something old goes out.

Sixth, *notice when the spaces you have already organized need attention and then re-order them.*

You will need to set time aside to go back through each space you have previously organized and re-order them.

Let's face it. The places you will have worked on (even with maintaining) will need to be freshened up a bit over the course of time. Re-ordering is just that, bringing the original order back to the space. Re-ordering is much, much easier than the first time you used *TOB* to gain the initial control over clutter. Since you already know what is assigned to each spot you have cleared out, re-ordering will be much easier.

The steps are the same as when you first began to use *TOB*. You will grab your box, a trash bag and a give away bag. **Gather** your items together. **Sort** each item out of your box into piles. **Assign** each item a place to live then put it there. Then continue to **Maintain** the order. The main difference between the first time you used your box on the space and this time is that it will take you considerably less time to re—order the same spot. Plus, you have the knowledge and habits of a whole year or so of using *TOB*. It will be easier to throw away things you don't need and easier to give away things you can't use anymore to someone else.

Since you will be taking steps along the way to keep an enormous amount of clutter from entering your home and you will be enlisting your family members' help, re-ordering will be much easier than it was originally. You may also discover that over the next year or so, you may want to re-organize a place in a way that is different than you had initially. This may be for any reason, such as, you realize that the items you initially decided to assign in that space would be better kept elsewhere. This happens often for me, because I find more efficient ways to re-do things time and time again. Sometimes, I just like change and variety. It is kind of like moving the furniture all around. A word of caution here though, areas that the whole family uses frequently are places I usually never change. This is simply because the family is used to where most things go, so it's best not to change things around that they use if you want to continue experiencing their help keeping your home tidy. The places I change around might be places where I keep my lotions, makeup, etc., or my own desk or bedroom.

So how do you know when it is time to re-order a space? That is the beauty of *TOB*. It is up to you to determine. You will know because the drawer will begin to look messy and cluttered or you may decide that you want to assign something else to the drawer or some other reason. For example, I knew it was time to re-order my office supply drawer when I began to notice the items which were assigned to the drawer were still in the drawer, but they were scattered and not in the particular container I had placed there for them. But since they were in the drawer they were assigned to I let it go for a while. I knew it was time when I needed a pencil, opened the drawer and grabbed one. The pencil point was broken off, so instead of sharpening it, like I should have, I put it right back because I was in a hurry and grabbed another pencil. Broken lead. Another one, broken. I realized, it was time. So, the next day, when I had about an hour, I grabbed my box and started working through the steps. I saw immediate results.

You might want to choose a particular season to re-order like the summer or fall. You may also wish to re-order during spring to coordinate with a time when you could hold a garage sale to eliminate your excess. Christmas is sometimes a good time to re-order when you feel your donations might be able to be more needed than perhaps another time of year.

If you choose to hold a garage sale, however, there are a few things you must do in order to ensure that your excess does not make its way back into your home. First, tell yourself and your family that when the garage sale items go out to the garage for the sale they will NOT be returning back inside your home in any way. When I ask my children if they have anything they wish to sell, I remind them of this garage sale family rule. It eliminates the change of heart that may occur at a later time when they decide they do not wish to sell that certain item. It helps tremendously to let yourself and your children know that if they sell ten or so items, the profit can be used to buy one or two nice new things that they would like to have.

Secondly, price your items to sell. The majority of garage sales I frequent are way out of my price range simply because the sellers think too much of their items. The way I see it is that the items I am choosing to sell would have been donated anyway, so any money I make is more than I would have if I had donated them. When people shop at my garage sales, they receive tremendous bargains. I know this because people attending tell me I have great prices on everything. When figuring how to price items, I usually set my prices on large items about one-eighth to one-tenth of the original cost new. For clothing, pairs of shoes and books, I usually price everything for a quarter. Pricing things in increments of 25, 50 cents or dollars makes the job of adding and dispensing change that much easier.

Third, clearly mark all prices and be willing to accept offers.

Fourth and most important, the more advertising you can do the better your results will be. Lots of signage and word of mouth will help make your sale a success.

Prior to your sale, decide what you will do with the leftovers. After our sales, my husband and I take any remaining large items to the curb for anyone to take for free (which is legal in our town, make sure you check with your local officials on the laws where you live). Then we load up the smaller items in boxes into our vehicle; take a trip to the local Salvation Army or Goodwill and drop off the items. Usually by morning the large items at the curb have been picked up. If not, we find someone with a truck (if they won't fit in our vehicle), load them up and make a second trip to the local charity.

Holding a garage sale is a lot of work, is time consuming and sometimes a royal pain, however, it is a good way to make a few extra bucks if you feel like putting forth the effort.

During re-ordering, if you choose to hold items for a sale, find a central place in your basement, attic or garage where you can shuttle the items after you have re-ordered. Make sure to hold your sale within a reasonable period of time after re-ordering otherwise you are just moving clutter around from one space to another and not really accomplishing anything.

For my friend, Tammy, her ultimate challenge was to be vigilant about keeping her table clean and clear for a full two weeks. I told her that I would be dropping by for quick announced and unannounced visits during those two weeks. My purpose for the visits was to see if her table looked the same way it did at the moment we had cleared and organized it. You can use this same method by telling a friend that you are using *TOB* and asking them to help hold you accountable to keeping your space neat. You can ask them to drop by occasionally during the two week maintaining period for motivation and encouragement.

This is where community can be used to motivate and encourage each other. Using *TOB* with a group of friends for maintaining, just as you may have done during sorting and assigning, is a fun way to succeed in organizing with others.

After I left Tammy, she called me later that evening upbeat and excited. "Everyone came home from school or work today and the first thing they commented on was how awesome the table looked." I could hear her smiling over the phone. I felt so happy that she had accomplished the task and that she was proud of it. She went on to say that her family enjoyed a beautiful, peaceful dinner at the table that evening. She even told me that everyone wanted to help her clear off and clean up the table to make it look like it did when they first came home.

I am very proud to say that each time I stopped by her home during that two—week period, knocked on the door and said, "Surprise!" her table looked as good as the day we had it cleared. After the course of two weeks she told me how, as the first one awake each morning, she felt at rest as she walked out into the dining room and saw the clear, neat table greeting her good morning. Tammy commented that her main motivation to keep up with maintaining was the feeling of calm and order she received along with the praise from her family. Over time, their help was less enthusiastic but she was training herself to put things back and working with her family to encourage them to do the same.

As you use *TOB*, you will begin to see exactly what you need to have in your life and what you do not. You will find your thinking changing from, "I need everything," to "I need some things."

You will find shopping will become easier because you will realize if it is something you feel you really want or need, then you can get it. If it is not, you can let it go and remember if you ever do really need it later on, you will enjoy buying it more then than you would now. If there is something that you decide you really must have, get it. However, when you bring it home, determine that you will find an old item already in your home to get rid of. The new item you brought home will be able to "replace" the old item you will give away.

I hope you are encouraged and motivated about how to maintain what you've organized after reading this chapter. It is much easier to stay decluttered after you have done all the initial hard work. It's just a matter of preventative maintenance and changing your thinking to accommodate your new lifestyle. See, you really can do it!

CHAPTER 9 SUMMARY

- ✓ The first time you use *TOB*, wait at least two weeks before moving on to a different space in order to ensure the habit of maintaining is formed
- ✓ Get into the habit of putting back items from where they are assigned when finished using — lead by example

✓ Ensure everyone in the household knows the function of each space and what is assigned to live there

✓ Train yourself to put things back

✓ Train other members of the household to put things back

✓ Before purchasing or accepting something from someone ask yourself if you really need it

✓ When you bring something new into your home get rid of something old

✓ Notice when spaces need to be decluttered and then use *TOB* to re-order them

✓ If you opt for a garage sale, do not bring any items back into your home after the completion of the sale

PART III. CONCLUSION

CHAPTER 10

THE ORGANIZING BOX SUMMARY

Well, first of all, I must say a hearty congratulation for reading this far in *The Organizing Box*. This means that you are serious about your desire to organize your home. As this book draws to a close and you know how *TOB* works, it's time for you to start using it to bring order to your spaces. You have heard of my success and others'. Hopefully you are encouraged and motivated to know that you can do it, too.

Remember there is no rush to complete. View each space that you complete as one step closer to finishing your entire home. Reference the pages that stood out to you and anything that particularly meant something to you.

The summaries I gave at the end of each chapter are in the following pages. You might want to think of them as a shortened guide to reference as you are actually working at using *TOB*. It is meant to be used only after you have read and understand *TOB* and all the things already discussed in detail from the beginning of this book. You will always have a quick reminder of the four sides that make up your organizing box since they will be written on each of the four sides of your box. Be sure to reference them if you forget what side comes next.

Thank you, fellow organizer, for reading. Thank you for letting me help you use *TOB* to beautify and simplify the spaces in your home. For additional organizing tips and motivations, or to contact me, please visit www.TheOrganizingBox.com.

CHAPTER SUMMARIES

<u>Chapter 1</u>

- ✓ *TOB* is a creative, practical approach to organizing the small spaces within your home one space at a time according to your schedule
- ✓ The four sides that support *TOB* are:
    1. Gathering
    2. Sorting
    3. Assigning
    4. Maintaining
- ✓ Read through the whole book before you begin

<u>Chapter 2</u>

- ✓ Organize at your own pace using whatever amount of time you have whether it is ten minutes or two hours
- ✓ You will use *TOB* on one small space at a time

Chapter 3

- ✓ Decide which area or room you want to organize first
- ✓ Decide in which small space within the area or room you will start

Chapter 4

- ✓ Gather a day and time you will organize — treat it as an appointment
- ✓ Look for time wherever you can fit it in
- ✓ Gather a box or plastic tote
- ✓ Gather two bags, a marker and some masking tape to use

Chapter 5

- ✓ Transfer all contents from your space into your box
- ✓ Vacuum, sweep or wipe out the bottom of the space and if you desire, line it

Chapter 6

- ✓ Sorting will be the most time consuming part of using *TOB*
- ✓ Sorting will be the most emotional part of using *TOB*
- ✓ Sorting will take some thought and decision making
- ✓ Learn to say no when it comes to collecting everything you are offered or tempted to make your own possession
- ✓ Decide to release the emotional attachment to your things
- ✓ Consider what you really need to save for future use

✓ Determine to be unaffected by the status others assign to you

Chapter 7

✓ Find a place to sort through your box

✓ Place labeled Trash Bag and Give Away Bag close by as you sort

✓ Go through each item in your box to sort by like items and place into piles

✓ Go through each pile looking for items to keep, give away or trash

✓ Ask questions about each item:

 1. Is it broken or useable?

 2. When was this item last used?

 3. Is this something I could do without because I will choose to keep another item instead?

 4. Do I have more than I really need of this item?

 5. Will I use this item if I choose to keep it?

 6. Can this item be one of a select few to go into a memory box?

✓ "Keep" items are items you use or will use

✓ "Give away" items have not been used within six months to a year and could be valuable to someone else

✓ "Trash" is anything broken or that no one else would want

✓ A memory box is a great way to keep a few items you don't

use but don't want to get rid of either

✓ The goal is to keep some but not all

Chapter 8

✓ Decide what items to assign to live in the organized space based on where it is located and what makes the most sense for it to hold

✓ Contain your piles in baggies, baskets or however you choose in order to fit their newly assigned "home"

✓ Place the items into their newly assigned space, making a list of containers or organizer items you may wish to purchase

✓ For the piles left on the table that are unassigned to this particular space, put the items into other places where they would somewhat fit

✓ If necessary, purchase baskets or create containers as soon as possible to help keep your piles within the new space orderly

Chapter 9

✓ The first time you use *TOB*, wait at least two weeks before moving on to a different space in order to ensure the habit of maintaining is formed

✓ Get into the habit of putting back items from where they are assigned when finished using — lead by example

✓ Ensure everyone in the household knows the function of each space and what is assigned to live there

✓ Train yourself to put things back

✓ Train other members of the household to put things back

✓ Before purchasing or accepting something from someone ask yourself if you really need it

✓ When you bring something new into your home get rid of something old

✓ Notice when spaces need to be decluttered and then use *TOB* to re-order them

✓ If you opt for a garage sale, do not bring any items back into your home after the completion of the sale

Made in the USA
Monee, IL
03 July 2021

72850433R00092